Shifting the Narrative

From Self-Doubt to Authentic Self-Worth

Anya M. Nolan

Please consult a licensed professional before attempting any techniques outlined in this book.

By reading this document, the reader agrees that under no circumstances is the author responsible for any losses, direct or indirect, that are incurred as a result of the use of the information contained within this document, including, but not limited to, errors, omissions, or inaccuracies.

Table of Contents

INTRODUCTION.. 1

CHAPTER 1: SELF-DOUBT AND SELF-WORTH 5

DECONSTRUCTING SELF-DOUBT 8
    Reaction Versus Response *10*
    Self-Doubt Is Not Simple Math *13*
    Your Problems and You Are Not Synonymous *14*
UNDERSTANDING WOUNDED SELF-WORTH 17
    Lack of Self-Love *19*
    Triggers From the Past *21*
    Childhood Trauma *22*
    Social Environment *24*
WHAT ARE YOUR BODY AND MIND TELLING YOU?...........................26
    Anger Is Telling You Something *26*
    Anxiety Is More Than Just Breathlessness *28*
    Guilt and Shame Are Dubious Friends *29*

CHAPTER 2: MYTHS OF SELF-WORTH.................................... 33

THE MYTHS SURROUNDING SELF-WORTH 36
    Myth #1: Having More Will Make You Feel Better *36*
    Myth #2: Your Body Shape Defines Your Worth *38*
    Myth #3: You're Not Okay if You're Not Exactly Like Them
    .... *41*
    Myth #4: You Are Nothing if Not Perfect at Everything... 43
    Myth #5: Your Worth Depends on Your Partner............. 44
DISCARDING MYTHS: STRATEGIES TO RECLAIM YOUR SELF-WORTH.....47
    Taking the Time to Know and Accept Yourself *47*
    Honest Evaluations but Avoiding Moral Judgments........ 51
    Body Positivity *53*
    Identifying Negative Relationship Patterns and Cultivating
    Healthy Ones *56*
    Letting Go of the Pressure to Be Perfect........................... *60*

CHAPTER 3: UNDERSTANDING IMPOSTER SYNDROME 63

DECODING IMPOSTER SYNDROME 63
  Is It So Simple? 66
  Why Do You Feel Like an Imposter? 67
THE TWO POLES OF IMPOSTER SYNDROME: BURNOUT AND
PROCRASTINATION 75
ACCESSING THE TRUTH BY REVERSING THE NARRATIVE 78

CHAPTER 4: CHALLENGING NEGATIVE SELF-TALK.................. 83

WHAT CAN NEGATIVE SELF-TALK SOUND LIKE? 86
STRATEGIES TO CHALLENGE NEGATIVE SELF-TALK 90
  Identifying Triggers and Externalizing Fears 90
  Checking Negative Emotions by Cultivating Positive Ones
  92
  Purposeful and Constructive Self-Talk 93
  Positive Affirmations Everyday 95
  Cognitive Behavioral Therapy Based Practices 97

**CHAPTER 5: REJECTION, RESILIENCE, AND THE GROWTH
MINDSET 103**

NAVIGATING REJECTIONS THROUGH A GROWTH MINDSET 104
  Nurturing a Growth Mindset 105
THE ROAD TO RESILIENCE 113

CHAPTER 6: DEVELOPING A STRONG SUPPORT SYSTEM 117

THE VICTORY 118
  The Turn Around 119
  The Return to the Track 121
STRONG SUPPORT SYSTEM: THE CATALYST FOR SELF-WORTH 122
HOW TO STRENGTHEN YOUR SUPPORT SYSTEM 126
  Instill the Sense of Connectedness 127
  Shift Your Perception of Self 127
  Reciprocity, Consideration, and Appreciation 128
  Diversify Your Circle 129
  Bring a Professional Onboard 130
  Let the Toxic Ones Go 131

CHAPTER 7: THREE GIFTS OF SELF-AWARENESS: GRATITUDE, FORGIVENESS, AND LETTING GO 135

PATHS TO SELF-AWARENESS...138
   Doing Nothing but Doing Everything: The Wisdom in Stillness 138
   Breathe In, Breathe Out...141
   Asking Questions and Observing Time 144
   Ground Your Body, Move Your Body...............................146
   Remembering You Are Nature 148
SELF-AWARENESS COMES BEARING GIFTS......................................150
   Gratitude 150
   Forgiveness..152
   Letting Go 155

CHAPTER 8: MAINTAINING STRONG SELF-WORTH: WELCOMING YOUR AUTHENTIC SELF 157

SELF-COMPASSION 159
TAKE THE WIN...160
UNDERSCORE THE ROLE OF REST 161
LET GO OF SELF-CENSORSHIP, EMBRACE YOLO 163
GO VISUAL...164
FEEL ALL THE FEELINGS..166
HONOR YOUR AUTHENTIC VALUES 167

CONCLUSION... 171

REFERENCES.. 175

Introduction

If I asked you to write a note to yourself about yourself that only you could privately read, what would be the first thing to pop up in your mind?

It is a seemingly innocuous question, but it is an important one. What we think about ourselves is critical. In the context of the question above, you can immediately be drawn to qualities that make you a wonderful person. Or you can simply think of your supposed flaws and become anxious about hiding them or fixing them. You and I may not choose to completely share what we think of ourselves with the people around us, but we almost always know it deep inside. And it decides how we show up in the world. Think of someone who looks like they have everything under control. They're great at their jobs and look phenomenal, but deep down, they battle with a negative self-image and insecurities. To the outside world, they appear perfect, but to themselves, perhaps worthless.

How do we make sense of such dichotomies? A simple way is to ask ourselves, what story about me am I telling myself? Regardless of what the outer world says about me, what do I believe about me? Answering these questions can show us what kind of self-image we have. Are we inspiring and loving ourselves for our efforts, or do we deride ourselves for even the smallest mistakes we make?

We spend half our lives trying to figure out what and where our place is in this world and another half perhaps making sense of how to get there. Eventually, our world throws up certain not-so-friendly situations in our faces. It is not a surprise then that we start having self-doubts. Am I capable of surviving, or do I even deserve the thing that I dream about? If you have also asked yourself these questions, you are not alone, my friend. We all do it at some point in our lives.

While some amount of self-doubt is needed, even necessary, a whole kilo of it doesn't do us any good! Continuously doubting ourselves is harmful to our general well-being. A persistent preoccupation with our worth dependent on the external world can cause us to spiral. It affects our personal and professional relationships and quality of life. It locks us in a pattern of self-hatred. Especially in our professional lives, we can feel like imposters constantly on guard lest someone realizes we don't deserve to be here. The pain of continuously being at war with ourselves is too much. It is well-documented that all this energy that goes into living in survival mode impacts our brains.

When we find ourselves in a mess, and our plans have turned to mush, it can feel like our dreams have shattered. A lot of unkind voices start sounding like prophecies of doom. The self-perpetuating cycle of negative talk gets to us, and before we know it, we start participating in it too. We are supposed to be our foremost cheerleaders, but we become unkind to ourselves. That is the thing with self-doubt. It is a dark maze with seemingly no way out.

But there is always a way out. We did not arrive here randomly. We followed a path that brought us here. And if we have come here, we can undoubtedly leave too. There is no mental prison that we build for ourselves that we cannot escape from. The idea is to allow ourselves to take the first step and keep walking ahead. Change can be daunting and by no means simple, but with a bit of help and a commitment to show up for ourselves every day, the road ahead becomes clearer. It starts with acknowledging and accepting ourselves for who we are and then understanding where our insecurities originate.

This book will reflect on the root causes of our struggles with low self-esteem and confidence. We will explore various tools and practical strategies that you can apply successfully to trace your way back to yourself and embrace your inherent self-worth. By the end of it, you will be able to identify the relationship between patterns of negative self-talk and low self-worth and start taking simple steps to reclaim your authentic sense of self.

It is like the art of Kintsugi. We are all incredible human beings not because we are flawless but because our scars make us who we are, and they bear witness to our journey.

It all begins with perspective. Let's shift the narrative together!

Chapter 1:

Self-Doubt and Self-Worth

Remember, you have been criticizing yourself for years and it hasn't worked. Try approving of yourself and see what happens. –
Louise L. Hay

Self-doubt is understood as uncertainty or lack of belief in one's capabilities to the extent that the effects are debilitating and hinder achieving one's goals, ultimately wounding our sense of self. Whatever its shape and degree, its result is the same in terms of wreaking havoc on our self-esteem. It is a vicious cycle that continuously makes us question our worth and place in the world. And when it is probed, it reveals itself to be anchored more in our negative thought patterns rather than actual objective truths. Self-doubt hinders your ability to take even those chances in life that may lead to growth.

Let me tell you a little story about Jonathan and his struggle with self-doubt.

Jonathan was a pianist with five years of experience in music production. He had performed a few gigs live at his local theater and usually loved to perform for his family and friends every two weeks. Everyone in the town considered him a brilliant artist and a rising star.

One night at a casual gathering of friends, he played a medley of seven different songs and ended on a high amidst people cheering him. However, he was not happy. As he got up from the piano, his friend Kelley noticed his dampened expression. She asked him if something was troubling him, and he replied in a defeated voice, "Yeah, I messed up some notes there like an idiot." She immediately recognized her friend's habit of overly critical self-assessment. Despite his many friends not noticing the slip-up at all and their fan-like adoration, Jonathan couldn't help but feel inadequate.

Three weeks later, he received an offer from a documentary film director to score his project. He was elated and immediately accepted the project. The director asked him to send a demo composition in a week. Jonathan got to work!

He sat at his piano and started playing some improvisations and taking notes. As he pondered over the subject matter of the film, he composed. Every few minutes, he would revisit the melody and cancel it out, thinking it didn't work and switching to a different idea. Hours passed, and he kept tearing up his papers one by one as he searched for the great idea.

Frustration started setting in, and he became distracted by his thoughts. Voices began swirling in his mind. *You haven't practiced enough. You don't have the skill. You are not creative enough. You should have had a demo soundtrack ready for such cases. You can't even come up with one catchy song; how will you score an entire film? What if they all see you are just an average artist*

Suddenly his chain of thought was broken, and he remembered the incident from three weeks ago. It pushed him further down the spiral, and he began thinking his performances were anyway sub-par. His minor slip, which happened weeks ago, became linked to his entire identity as a pianist in the present moment. *Maybe I should give up for now and wait until I am prepared*, he thought. His heart raced, and he felt breathless now, and it seemed like the walls of his room were squeezing in on him. He felt sure that he was not ready for such a project just yet. *He did not have the skill yet.* He quickly reached out for his laptop, emailed the director, made some excuse, thanked him for the opportunity, and bowed out of the project altogether. This wasn't the first time something like this had happened.

When his disaster-mongering thoughts eased and the gravity of what he had done dawned on him, another spiral began. This time, self-loathing spiraled. *Why must I be like this*, he wondered and started giving himself counter-arguments. He now started to feel the pangs of letting this opportunity pass him by. Surely he could have managed something. Even if this would not have been the greatest work of his life, it was a start. *How will I climb the summit if I don't take the first step? How can I make a warm cup of tea if I don't pour the water, huh? I am doomed to repeat the same mistakes over and over again*! He started to feel like a coward. He knew well that his constant doubts about himself had made him sabotage his growth on a few more occasions. And this made him feel ashamed.

We will come back to Jonathan again a little bit later and determine if what we learn can be of help to him. But first, let us see what really happened here. A musician with a fair bit of experience as well as praise allowed himself to be controlled by his anxiety and self-doubt, which in turn, made him feel even more anxious and powerless.

The natural question is, why did this happen? Why does it happen to any of us? You may have noticed that self-doubt can grip even those people who are awesome at what they do. They may have a supportive group of friends, family, or colleagues and still grapple with crippling anxiety. To answer this, we need to understand the root of where the problem stems from.

Deconstructing Self-Doubt

I encourage you to take a moment and do this short activity. Grab a pen and paper. Write down the worst memory you have of someone criticizing you for a task that truly made you question your abilities. It can be anything ranging from making a presentation for work or cooking a particular dish, or singing a song, anything that you were harshly criticized for. Note down three things: the emotions you felt when it happened, your thoughts about it now, and does it hold any significance for you today concerning the performance of that task. Take a few minutes and come back with your responses.

Chances are that the response you note down for the first question centers around being hurt. Anger, shame, disappointment, and guilt can all be thought of as connected with being hurt. When someone criticizes us, we feel a kind of rejection. A critique signals that something has happened that has made us not fit to be accepted. And, as we know, being accepted is linked to a crucial social need we all have as is the need to belong and feel safe. So, when this feeling is triggered, our sense of being safe gets questioned. Naturally, our first instinct is to think that *we* did something wrong; *we* are the problem. This is the antecedent of what becomes chronic self-doubt—the act of discounting our skills and turning on ourselves.

Now usually, when this initial feeling of being rejected subsides, we can reason with ourselves, and our problem-solving mental apparatus kicks in. We can make a calm assessment of what went wrong and move ahead from there. If this is the case, your answer to the second and third questions can be on the lines of not being affected by the incident that much in the present and the criticism not negatively impacting your performance today, except for you being careful or better at performing the said task.

But sometimes, this is not the case. If you have found that your answer to the latter two questions fills you up with strong negative emotions and anxiety, and this memory comes up to the surface every time a new opportunity to do something similar presents itself, you might be locked in a pattern of reacting rather than responding.

Understanding the difference between the two is key to understanding self-doubt.

Reaction Versus Response

A reaction is something instant. Imagine walking into a room and your friend jumping up from behind, giving you a jump scare. You may scream back at them or may even punch them. Now, that doesn't mean you hate your friend, obviously! These are just the body's reactions to being caught off-guard in a threat-like situation. But *responding* to a situation is different in the sense that you take some time, understand the situation, and then respond. It is a well-thought-of thing.

Consider a different example. Suppose you and your friend have applied for an internship position together, but there is only one slot for the intake. They get selected and call you to give you the news in excitement. You feel sad and frustrated, so you simply congratulate them hurriedly and get off the call. Later that day, you meet them with a box of cupcakes and a congratulations card and put on your best face forward. You tell them that you're happy for them even though you are sad about not making it through (which is a natural emotion). Now *that* is a response.

In this situation, you could have *reacted* with anger, said something insensitive to your friend without meaning it, or maybe lashed out against the unfairness of life. But you took the time not to say anything instantly and rather dealt with the situation thoughtfully. You acknowledged your emotions and figured out a way to be authentic without denying how you felt.

But what has this got to do with self-doubt? When someone is locked in a pattern of reacting rather than responding, they function instinctively. Think about how we react in situations of fight-or-flight. There is a wide body of research that documents this relationship between stress, the autonomic nervous system, and trauma, for example, Bessel van der Kolk's *The Body Keeps the Score* and Dr. Nicole LePera's *How to Meet Your Self* (van der Kolk, 2014; LePera, 2022). Our body's autonomic nervous system makes us react to danger even before our conscious rational brain can make sense of the threat and analyze it.

Serious self-doubt can trigger a tornado of anxiety, making us interpret a situation as more threatening than it actually is. It is threatening, precisely because we feel afraid of losing control over the outcome. We take an experience from the past and use that memory to remind ourselves of how we failed to achieve something. We react to that fear by preserving ourselves from such a situation of powerlessness. This manifests in the form of holding ourselves back. *If I don't try, I cannot fail.* This perspective gels with self-doubt to unhinge us from our reality and makes us act from a position of feeling that we are not worthy enough.

Self-doubt, then, is a reaction to our fears and anxieties about ourselves. It is a reaction to the narrative we tell ourselves. We maximize our flaws and minimize our qualities. Our friend Jonathan was also reacting to his inner voice belittling his achievements. He blew his minor mistake out of proportion and did not take into account his creative ability to work hard at all. He forgot to be his biggest ally and stood in the way of realizing his dreams.

At this point, one can be inclined to think that so far, so good. As long as we get out of our heads and stop the self-sabotage, we can merrily go on achieving our goals. If only things were so easy, life was fair, and the world had unicorns!

Self-Doubt Is Not Simple Math

Simplifying the problem of self doubt can result in trivializing the problem. The story is not so linear, with an absolute black-and-white distinction. Breaking our thought patterns is no child's play, and it certainly does not come easy. Often the acknowledgment of the problem does not automatically mean its translation into a solution. And people with self-doubt can be convinced of their inadequacy. You cannot act on something if you don't have the conviction, and if your conviction tells you that you are not worth it, it becomes increasingly difficult to believe otherwise.

This is where our perspective on things plays an important role. Let's go back to the phrase we saw above. *If I don't try, I cannot fail.* But this can also be restated in another manner: *If I don't try, I cannot succeed.* A self-confident person and someone struggling with self-doubt will read this sentence differently. A self-confident person will read it as *I can fail if I try, and trying is worth it.* They will emphasize that though the outcome may not turn out exactly how they planned, they can never be truly at a loss for trying because they gain experience and learn, making them more equipped to try again with a higher chance of success. They attach a greater value to collecting unique experiences. However, a person with self-doubt will fixate on the *I can fail* part. For them, the emphasis is on failure and an urgent need to avoid it as a strategy of self-preservation from within. They get trapped in negative preconceived notions of how things will necessarily unfold.

You can see how our perspectives color the outer world and our experience of reality. Our skewed perspective can create a harmful feedback loop where:

- We think of ourselves as not capable enough, keeping us stuck in inaction and avoidance.

- Inaction, in turn, fuels the belief of not being capable enough because the fear of failure never allows us to try something enough times to gain confidence.

It keeps going on and on, and soon we conclude that the problem must lie with us. That somehow, we are responsible for every bad thing that happens to us. This could not be farther from the truth. While it is not something we deliberately choose to put ourselves through, we can consciously try to devise roadmaps to steer us away from it.

Your Problems and You Are Not Synonymous

Feeling like you are the cause of everything bad happening in your life is like being pulled in by a mental quicksand. It is a quagmire of thoughts that closes in upon itself to suffocate you. It hides the more sinister roots of the problem from view to give a false sense of accountability. Self-assessment and accountability for our actions are no doubt essential elements of growing in life, but like everything else, these are susceptible to distortion. Our sense of accountability can be bamboozled.

Imagine blaming someone for carrying their wallet with them and getting mugged or having legs for stepping in gum. It sounds absurd. Getting mugged is an external problem, with the mugger being at fault. Stepping on gum is just an unfortunate accident or the universe being funny at our expense! The point is bad things can happen to us *without* our active involvement. Our behavior is both a cause of things and a result of things, existing in a complex symbiotic relationship between our internal and external worlds.

Our behavior does not evolve in isolation. Everything from our childhood to social conditioning and biological factors shapes how we behave. The same is true for self-doubt and anxiety. There is no single unified theory that can provide an exact cause for it. Our genetic makeup, life experiences, the parenting style of our parents, and our environment all play a role in deciding the degree to which we feel anxious (Trenton, 2021). Therefore, it does not make sense to hound ourselves for our anxieties and fears. They are clearly shaped by things beyond our control, and yet, self-doubt does exactly that to us.

Think of it like distinguishing between you as a person and the things you possess. I can *have* an ice cream in my possession, but I am *not* an ice cream myself! Similarly, I am a person who has some problems, but I myself am not the problem.

We must realize that the language we use has the potential to either imprison us or liberate us. By framing the issue in this way, we can externalize the issue and free ourselves from our harsh, judgmental tendencies. We can avoid linking our character to our problems.

Say it with me; *I am not a horrible person for having problems, just a human being. And I am perfectly capable of facing them by taking control and seeking help.* We can try and find a balance between making life happen *for* us by consciously directing our efforts and enjoying life as it is happening *to* us by letting things unfold in their time instead of worrying.

We cannot make complete sense of the impact of self-doubt without talking about self-worth. Chronic self-doubt often overlaps with wounded self-esteem, and exploring the relationship between self-doubt and self-worth sheds some light on how it becomes a self-perpetuating cycle. An interesting study published by Hermann et al. (2002) empirically demonstrates the relationship between self-doubt and self-esteem, noting that people with higher and consistently enduring self-doubt are more likely to have a declined sense of self-esteem, and they are likely to be more sensitive in recognizing their thoughts around self-doubt.

Understanding Wounded Self-Worth

Have you ever found yourself walking out of a situation where you thought you deserved something better? What about walking out of a friendship where your friend does not value your time and plans and takes you for granted? Do you wonder how we assess other people's treatment of us as not being correct? That is because we all have an innate sense of what it means to be treated fairly or unfairly. And that sense comes from our sense of self-esteem or self-worth.

When we respect ourselves enough to know what we deserve and how we want to be treated, we make changes in our lives that align with our self-worth. If you're confident in your worth, you can leave that toxic relationship that does not fulfill you. You can sing that song you love in a karaoke bar. You can wear that lovely dress. You can pretty much do anything you really care about and create an environment of love and support around you. *You don't need anyone's permission to be the vibrant you.*

But why do we sometimes end up keeping ourselves in a place where we consistently feel devalued? Struggling with low self-esteem can cause us to lose trust in our inherent value and keep us shackled to a miserable place. Wounded self-worth can make us feel trapped inside a room with no key. But the most devastating impact it has on us is to take away our will to walk out even when the door is open. Because, to a person with low self-worth, escaping does not feel like a possibility. They can feel like nothing can change, and nothing ever will, for all times to come. And *that* is the most heartbreaking thing.

Imagine women who are unable to leave an abusive marriage. As Jason Whiting explains, they may expect that their love and efforts can change another person by showing enough loyalty and care, or they may feel they deserve it. Sometimes, the trauma of abuse can make them terrified of leaving, as survivors are often subjected to physical threats if they dare leave (Whiting, 2016).

It doesn't have to be a case as severe as domestic violence, but even in day-to-day life, low self-esteem can make it difficult to make choices aimed at our well-being. Choosing to live happily and have meaningful connections with people are intrinsic to our sense of self-worth. But because we operate from a mindset of a lack of self-worth, whatever little love and affection we get from outside, we make peace with it. It is a compromise that we enter into thinking this situation or person is not ideal, but what else, if not *this*?

There is no way to exactly identify the moment when someone's self-worth takes a hit, but most likely, it is an ongoing process with multiple trigger points.

Lack of Self-Love

Often when the layers of low self-worth are peeled away, we find a lack of self-love. Not only do we love ourselves insufficiently, but we also even think that we don't *deserve* to be loved. But why must someone feel they don't deserve to be loved?

We live in a world that operates on the concepts of good and bad, constantly hammering away at us to be a better person. We all want to be successful in life, don't we? As we grow up, we start learning about the connection between certain behaviors and the feeling of deserving love. Being loved becomes a reward for being good.

Now, who tells us if we are good or not? Other people tell us that, be it in the form of our parents asking us to behave or societal norms shaping our sense of morality. And, since we are social creatures, we depend on being accepted in society to feel happy. It makes us feel like we matter. It is easy to love ourselves when we are cherished by the people around us.

But let me ask you, why are we so susceptible to other people's judgments and opinions about us? How is it that we tend to act and feel in ways similar to the people around us? Think of a baby learning to make sounds before speaking coherently or bursting into laughter listening to another person's funny laugh! There is science behind it!

Bessel van der Kolk beautifully explains in *The Body Keeps the Score* that we have mirror neurons which are responsible for our ability to empathize with others and account for many other behavioral phenomena like imitation, synchronizing our actions with others, and language development. But they are also responsible for us absorbing other people's negative emotions (van der Kolk, 2014).

Needless to say, this means we are indeed affected by other people around us. Our modern technology-driven society makes it easier to expose ourselves to external judgment. And sometimes, this runs the risk of internalizing what they think about us. When this goes too far, we can, for different reasons, start feeling we are not worthy of love.

When we tell this to ourselves enough times, we start believing it and forget that no matter what, we deserve our unconditional love. The before-mentioned idea of being our foremost cheerleaders in life gets buried somewhere deep inside. We replace external negative voices with our own, ridiculing ourselves. We shall talk about negative self-talk in Chapter 4, but it is important to recognize it as a significant sign of a lack of self-love.

Triggers From the Past

The past serves as a repository of knowledge and functions as a manual for survival. But it can also keep us stuck there, especially if there are major emotional upheavals existing within us. When we go through a challenging experience that does not meet our expectations and makes us feel doubtful of our capabilities or worthless, it can become a trigger for us in the future. Whether or not it qualifies as trauma, the memory reminds us of the unpleasantness. These triggers act as a pre-programmed mechanism that can influence our thought process into believing the past outcome will be repeated. This pattern of associating our past experiences with the expectation of the present harms our self-worth as it can be a painful reminder of our perceived worthlessness.

For example, being asked a question in an interview that you don't know the answer to can be embarrassing. When this embarrassing experience is repeated in your mind, it can turn into an uncontrollable spiral and affect your performance in subsequent interviews. The more it happens, the more negative experiences you collect, making the whole process of facing an interview a trigger point.

Van der Kolk (2014) writes about our brain's fear center, the amygdala, being triggered by memories of the past or even objects that are connected to a traumatic event from the past. As the amygdala is triggered, a series of stress hormones are released, causing physiological changes like increased heartbeat and blood pressure. He explains how trauma makes distinguishing between the past and present difficult because different parts of the brain capture various aspects of a traumatic experience. As a result, we can lose the ability to form a rational and coherent narrative around it. The consequence is reliving it again and again, only in a progressively worse manner.

Childhood Trauma

An unhappy childhood and neglect are generally accepted as the most significant reason for low self-worth. Parents that are uninvolved or overly critical of their children create an environment of fear and anxiety. Children feel and observe everything and pick up verbal and non-verbal cues. In that case, neglect can signal a sense of being unimportant and unrecognized. As Suzanne Lachmann describes, "Feeling unrecognized can result in the belief that you are supposed to apologize for your existence" (Lachmann, 2013).

On the other hand, a life-threatening event or continuous abuse (both physical and mental), whether by a parent, family member, or a stranger, can deeply traumatize a child for life.

According to research, trauma can cause neurobiological issues in a child and changes in brain function. It has a long-term impact on cognition and *self-image*, which can spill into adulthood and make people prone to a host of psychological conditions ranging from substance abuse to mood irregularities and difficulties in interpersonal relationships (Dye, 2018).

But childhood experiences don't have to be extreme to cause self-esteem issues. Sometimes, what counts as a typical insignificant event for adults, can leave deep scars on a child's psyche. Let me tell you about little Josie.

Josie was eight when her dad took her to an amusement park. She loved the bumper car ride and always wanted to try it. He got her a ticket, and she stood in the queue, waiting her turn. When her turn came, she ran to her favorite blue car, but another kid jumped in with his sister before she could get in. She looked around but found all the cars occupied, so she decided to wait for the next round.

Suddenly she heard someone call her a loser. It was the same kid who jumped into her car with his sister. Josie felt embarrassed, and her ears flushed red as her eyes grew moist. She decided to run away from there. Her father caught up behind her and yelled at her for being a poor sport. He expressed his disappointment by passing off a rude remark about her not understanding the value of his hard-earned money as she let the ticket go to waste. She cried all the way back home in her father's car. She felt emotionally unsafe as no words of consolation were spoken to her. She felt like a horrible person for making her father angry unintentionally and, indeed, a loser for letting the other kid take her place.

Years later, she was surprised when she recounted this long-suppressed memory in talk therapy. It came as a revelation to her that her deep-seated unease with being emotionally vulnerable around people and her low self-worth was rooted in this memory. Listening to unkind words from someone you love and look up to can damage your self-confidence. More so when it is someone we count on to have our back in tough times. Of course, Josie's father loved her with all he had, and she knew it, but the emotional experience of that eight-year-old girl imprinted something in her psyche that was not very easy to erase.

Everyone's childhood experience is different, but trauma is dangerous for our overall health. Often trauma survivors can assign blame to themselves, which plays a significant role in causing self-worth issues. It is extremely important to realize that whatever happens to you as a child is never your fault.

Social Environment

External factors, such as our social environment, are as much responsible for causing self-worth issues as internal factors. As noted before, humans don't evolve in isolation from the broader context in which they live.

Our immediate relationships, socio-political structures, and exposure to different kinds of audio-visual media play a crucial role in what we grow up aspiring to and believing in. Even issues like access to resources and opportunities, impacted by different local, national, and global forces, can be sinister players in our story.

The following are some major, but by no means exhaustive, environmental causes affecting our sense of self-worth:

- unsafe and toxic public environment like bullying and ragging in schools

- online ragging or cyberbullying

- conflict-ridden home environment

- denial of personal autonomy by others

- violation of personal space, time, and energy by others

- absence of a strong support system

- discriminations based on gender, race, ethnicity, and other identity-based factors

- constant comparisons with others

- media representations of desirability and undesirability, especially via social media

- dealing with mental health issues

These factors can combine in varying degrees to make us feel overwhelmed and doubt ourselves, raising the familiar question of being good enough.

At this point, it is essential to ask, is self-doubt and low self-worth only a psychological phenomenon? Can it affect our physical body? The answer is yes, and the next section explores the signs that our body gives us.

What Are Your Body and Mind Telling You?

Identifying the trigger points of low self-worth can help us understand our behavior instead of suppressing unwanted emotions. Our body stores trauma memories, and we can use the cues it gives to gain some insight into how it reacts under all the stress caused by low self-worth. Emotions are not just a matter of how we feel mentally but also physically.

Anger Is Telling You Something

Anger is often the most powerful emotion we have. Many know its dangers and adverse effects, like uncontrollable rage leading to disastrous outcomes. Still, anger by itself serves a protective purpose as a defense mechanism. It asks us to stand up for ourselves when something we care about is at risk.

But can anger be useful and creative? Can it be used for a deeper purpose? Does it reveal something to us?

Think of an incident that made you extremely angry at some point in your life. Maybe someone overtook you dangerously at an intersection while you were driving carefully. Or perhaps your boss promoted someone else over you because they had contacts high up in the management. It could be any incident, but there will be a sense of unfairness attached to it. The more you probe, the more you can figure out that we get angry when we feel something is unfairly taken away from us or denied to us, which hurts us. It is like an ultimate weapon against something we perceive as unjust.

However, when we struggle with self-doubt and low self-worth, we can be furious toward ourselves for not being better and toward the world for feeling sad or rejected. This negative self-talk is the manifestation of our anger directed toward us. It is not just a result but also a symptom of a deeper struggle within ourselves. It makes us more sensitive to criticism and contributes to an increased likelihood of getting angry. And inwardly directed anger can lead to self-harm (Golden, 2023).

An interesting study published by Renouf and Harter (1990) researched the link between low self-worth, depression, and anger in adolescents and found that anger and low self-worth are both experienced as a combined effect of depression. They suggested a strong correlation between struggles of self-worth and feeling *mad* at ourselves.

Sitting with our anger quietly without judgment can be an enlightening experience and can tell us something about where it stems from. The next time you feel baffled by your rage, try listening in. Maybe it is trying to draw your attention to yourself, asking you to love yourself a little bit more!

Anxiety Is More Than Just Breathlessness

Remember Jonathan? Remember his breathlessness as he felt trapped in his negative thoughts? He was experiencing an anxiety attack as his thoughts took control of his situation.

Have you ever wondered why anxiety causes an increased heart rate most commonly? It can be understood as an intense feeling of fear or terror that causes functional disruptions in normal everyday life. The physical manifestations of anxiety can look similar, but each experiences a mix of standard and unique anxiety symptoms. Often the most reported ones include an increased heart rate, hyperventilation, breaking into sweats, feeling exhausted, and a perceptible change in sleep pattern (Mayo Clinic, 2018).

The feeling of exhaustion especially stands out because so much of your energy goes into surviving by avoiding distressing situations and anxiety triggers. It zaps out the strength to do things that are otherwise enjoyable to a person.

So, what does it all tell you?

We know self-doubt makes us underestimate ourselves, usually because of an overall crisis with our sense of self. If we look closely, anxiety related to our performance in the world stems from the constant questioning of our worth and a negative belief that we will mess up even the simplest things.

Sowislo and Orth (2013) have conducted a meta-analysis of 77 existing and 18 studies on depression and anxiety, respectively, revealing a link between self-esteem and anxiety. Their analysis shows a symmetric relationship between low self-esteem and anxiety. This means that both have a mutually reciprocal impact on each other.

If you have struggled with bouts of crippling anxiety, be gentle with yourself. Hang in there. Have faith that you can slowly but steadily take back control.

Guilt and Shame Are Dubious Friends

What? Dubious friends? Yes, you read that right!

Normally, guilt and shame function as needles of our internal moral compass. But we can be lost if our compass starts to act funny. There is a relationship between mistakes and guilt. Guilt can keep us grounded and urge us to be considerate of our fellow beings. If we hurt someone, guilt can push us to rectify our actions and be better in the future. And shame acts as an internal filter as we mold our behavior so that we are not ashamed of how we project ourselves in the world.

Guilt and shame, however, can also paralyze us when it comes to prioritizing our needs. Self-doubt not only manifests as undirected anger and anxiety about our perceived shortcomings, but it also sends us on a light-speed guilt trip for not living up to some abstract and unreasonable standard of perfection.

For example, are you trying to eat healthily and thinking of pastry? Bam, guilt trip. Trying to please everyone? Bam, someone is unhappy, guilt trip. Your brother is asking for money, but you are low on cash? Double bam, guilt trip for not showing up for the family. Because we already feel worthless, we quickly ascribe faults to ourselves without checking if they are warranted. In many cases, this horrible feeling of being ashamed is uncalled-for. Responsibilities do not mean unconditional availability.

Budiarto and Helmi (2021) note that guilt causes self-devaluation and lowers our image in our eyes. It is debilitating because such devaluation can cause us emotional pain. We can think then guilt and shame are our dubious friends, and they don't always reflect the truth about ourselves.

The next time you feel guilty about something, ask yourself, are you really at fault? Have you caused any harm to someone, or are you just guilty of taking up space? Because if it is the latter, don't feel guilty, as the world is big enough for all of us, and we shouldn't be restricting ourselves from a fuller expression of ourselves.

All the signs that our body gives us a hint toward the need to slow down and reflect. Understanding the causes of self-doubt and low self-worth, as they apply to you individually, is a journey that takes time and will not happen in one day. But it is not impossible! Armed with insights, you can take the first step toward transforming your life. You can have the safety of knowing your worth.

As we move ahead, it's imperative to realize that a distorted self-image and decline in self-worth can result from many myths perpetuated by flawed representations of worth. Dispelling these myths becomes necessary for building confidence and reclaiming your worth. Now that we are done with the seriously dense conversation of self-doubt and self-worth, let's dispel some myths together!

Chapter 2:

Myths of Self-Worth

Did you know that there are more than 35,000 *published* studies about self-esteem (Bleidorn et al., 2016)? Yeah!

Some of these studies are truly cross-sectional, taking into account the role played by gender, age, and culture in people's opinions about themselves. For example, the study by Bleidorn et al. (2016) takes evidence from 48 countries to show that despite some variations, males generally have higher self-esteem than females and that self-esteem can increase with the transition from adolescence to middle age.

So even when you feel like a solitary hermit struggling with the gut-wrenching effects of low self-worth, you are not alone.

But if there is so much information on self-worth, why don't we all just educate ourselves and become free of this burden? The simple answer is that along with information, there is a lot of misinformation too. The Internet and the ever-faster-growing networks of communication technologies expose us to so much at once that we can't help but feel overwhelmed. Why? Because much of what gets disseminated creates this crazy race for attaining this perfect aesthetic of life that we should all be running after. And they permeate all areas of life.

Take Instagram, for example. You open it and get bombarded by a million advertisements showing you:

- this aesthetically appealing stationary that you must have if you want to journal

- that perfect holiday you must go to, especially with that perfect white sandy beach to rejuvenate (lest you remain wretched for the rest of your life)

- that superb diet plan you need to follow if you want to flaunt six-pack abs or that expensive keratin treatment if you want silky smooth hair (as if having texture is a sin)

- that perfect job to make you rich quick

- this insurance, this plan, that house

- that perfect class to make you an expert in a skill

- that color, this sound, that food, this experience...

It doesn't end. Having all of this is not bad per se. But feeling like your life depends on it is indeed problematic. The problem lies in accepting the story that external sources tell you: what *you should desire* and what you *need* to have in order to be truly happy. Anyone with a marketing job will tell you how the demand-supply chain works. Manufacture a need, create a dream, and sell your product! Marketing doesn't seem so innocent, eh?

We get so enchanted by what we see that we forget to ask, do I really depend on all this? What are the standards portrayed here? Are they sustainable and true in the long run? Will they change me and solve my problems? Many people have misconceptions about their self-worth because of this.

While some of these misconceptions are caused by social media, news channels, the entertainment industry, and the internet, not all are. Some misunderstandings are caused by factors that we saw in the previous chapter. Interactions with our environment, early childhood experience, friends, and co-workers, shape our perception of how worthy we are. Constant comparison with whatever is out there in the world can make us think we need to conform to it. And if we make a mistake or fall short of this standard, we lose all right to be content. But imagine a rose not wanting to exist because it was not a daisy! Quit with the platitudes, you say, but life's truths come in mind-boggling absurdities. And the most significant revelations affirm what we already know deep inside.

Growing and evolving sure is part of life but change just for the sake of change is not meaningful. Yes, happiness can come from successfully facing challenges, changing habits that hold you down, and fulfilling your dreams, but it cannot come from doing all those things to prove a point to someone else. Because, newsflash, they may not care. What happens then? Do all your efforts and everything you've worked for suddenly lose meaning? No!

All that growth does not become untrue. It adds to you as a human being. Only you can live your life, and only you can do it right! Everything and everyone else is just confetti.

The biggest myth of self-worth, then, is that it comes and is sustained from the outside. It takes various forms but always comes back to this: *you.*

Let's have a look at some of the forms these myths can take and break them down.

The Myths Surrounding Self-Worth

Myth #1: Having More Will Make You Feel Better

When Clara was young, her cousin had a big tent house. She asked her parents if she could get one too. They said yes. When she was in college, her friend had a beautiful butterfly tattoo, and she got the same one. When she started working, almost half of her salary went into buying glittery stuff she saw online, and she became a shopaholic. She always experienced joy in getting herself new things, but it subsided within a day until she could find another fix.

In contrast, Ronny came from an economically challenged family and saw his classmates show off their new birthday presents yearly. He understood the situation and never pressured his parents into buying stuff for him but often thought to himself, one day, when I have enough, I will buy myself everything I want. Ronny became successful and owned three cars, the best watches, and the best suits. He still could not relinquish this feeling of being less from his childhood.

One of the myths we all easily harbor is that having more things will make us feel better, but it doesn't actually do that. Wanting more is anchored in the knowledge of scarcity, of not having something. We think having more things makes us cool or quirky, but we're already all those things if we just take a moment to see that. Think of the million brands advertising their products on the lines of *superior products for a better you!* Having or not having things is more than simply possessing them. If those things don't hold any significant meaning for us, we'll still be miserable.

Consiglio and Osselaer (2022) explain how consumption and exposure to brands on social media with unattainable lifestyle standards can highlight a difference between actual self-image and an inflated self-image, which in turn, can lower self-esteem.

Self-worth does not come from having more. At the end of the day, you're going to be living with yourself. So, even if outwardly you can uphold some standard that does not speak to who you are, you will always know it internally. And that is the whole point! If you know you are worthy, which you are, as every human is, you will never need those outward things to remind yourself or others of your value.

Myth #2: Your Body Shape Defines Your Worth

This myth is perhaps the most dangerous one of all and can drive people to an unhealthy standard of self-censoring.

Have you ever noticed yourself posing a certain way in pictures or selfies? You know which angle will hide that flaw you are so worried about. Or perhaps you don't click photos of yourself at all. Maybe you use a filter before posting yourself online? There are countless stories of people, especially women, who have looked at themselves in the mirror and thought they didn't have the ideal body type. I am too fat; I am too skinny; I am too short; I am too tall; I don't have a toned body; I have a body that's too toned, and whatnot!

With everything human, a comparison of our body types is inevitable. But the constant bombardment of unrealistic beauty standards causes grave harm to our sense of self. So much so that young adolescents also struggle with body image issues. We end up objectifying ourselves, and when we don't match the golden standard, whatever that is, we feel a crushing sense of defeat. We withdraw into our shells, and that affects our relationships. It can make us deny ourselves so many wonderful things, even something as simple as dancing freely!

While social media cannot be blamed as an utterly evil machine, it can act like one if not used with care. Even though our times have seen a rise in promoting body positivity trends, we need to catch up in actually making everyone feel at home in their own skin. It is no wonder that for the longest time, the only thing we saw everywhere, from movies and comics to advertisements of the most mundane things, was a particular representation of the perfect body.

But social media differs from earlier forms of media precisely in its intimate and immediate nature. With newer updates to enhance experience and participation with peers, the constant influx of images can lead to body dissatisfaction and body surveillance. The experience with social media is also linked to a higher possibility of eating disorders, promoted by a desire to fit the projected body standard (Santarossa & Woodruff, 2017).

Body dysmorphia is a serious mental health condition, and it is emotionally draining when someone continuously worries over flaws that others may not notice at all. Body image issues can drive people to extremes hoping to feel good about themselves, but often, it can have the opposite result. As for body size, losing or gaining weight for anything other than health reasons is fraught with difficulties. Firstly, if you do it for others, there will always be something else that others will find to poke around or judge. Secondly, if they judge you for your weight, they're already superficial, and should you change yourself for someone else's superficiality? Do it if you feel that is what you want, but your body type and shape do not tell anyone whether you're a good person or not. Quiet that voice that tells you otherwise!

It is essential to realize that there is absolutely nothing wrong with wanting to look attractive but looking great is such a subjective thing. You may spend hours trying to look a certain way, but you're already dapper to the people who care! I know it sounds effortless, but we know it is not. Simply thinking positively about ourselves is not going to cut it. But consciously unlearning the beauty myth is rewarding once you realize everything that you are already makes you unique.

Myth #3: You're Not Okay if You're Not Exactly Like Them

Have you ever felt like the odd one out in a group because they share a particular common interest that you don't? Technically, groups are based on commonality but not always. And not all members of a group share all things in common. Think of it like a mosaic. You can make a stunning art piece using varying sizes of glass pieces, different in colors and shapes. You don't need a group of perfectly identical glass pieces to achieve a marvelous piece of work.

Yet sometimes, there is this need to fit in. It can set you on a path to seek external validation and approval. But seeking approval is a dicey game because you constantly keep checking in with the person whose approval you are seeking to reassure yourself of being in a safe position. By safe position, I mean a place of acceptance where your views align with the views of others by being non-threatening to them and, therefore, by not inviting any conflict or retaliation.

Alienation from our peers is a debilitating feeling. Not belonging can be a lonely and scary experience, dealing a cruel blow to our sense of self. You can end up asking yourself, what am I if not a part of something? Sometimes this can indeed foster a sense of being inadequate and disconnected. But it can push you into showing up for things you don't enjoy. This is a slippery slope because it can quickly become a people-pleasing act. The effect it produces serves to dilute your authentic voice

People with people-pleasing tendencies have a hard time setting boundaries and maintaining them. It further damages your self-worth if you choose to agree with others over conflicting values just to keep the peace and not offend anybody. The outcome can be especially harsh when you cannot reconcile your behavior with what you actually stand for.

But if they saw you stand up for yourself, won't you be left alone then? If the answer is yes in your case, perhaps you are better off letting go of people who would not allow you your space. Sure, human relations are built on care, but they are also built on reciprocity. And, even if some people have more of a giving nature, there is a difference between being giving and what is colloquially known as energy vampires.

Figuring out more about your niches can be an empowering experience. It can be like your personal adventure of finding something about yourself that sets you apart. We all have that one thing that is just ours and that can fulfill us from within. And instead of running away from it, embracing it can do wonders for our self-image. It can build not only resilience but also confidence.

Sometimes, it is okay not to belong! Just because someone doesn't understand your choices doesn't mean they are right about them. It is not other people's perception of your happiness that determines your happiness, it is your own. You're certainly okay if you're not *exactly* like them.

Myth #4: You Are Nothing if Not Perfect at Everything

Self-worth is not about being exceptionally brilliant at everything. Or even brilliant at one thing consistently. Even the most groundbreaking experts in different fields have had years of experience with failure.

Low self-worth can make it incredibly challenging for people to accept failure and get back up. Because you consistently subject yourself to scrutiny, anything less than perfect comes out as outrightly horrible. An overly critical self-perception cannot only harm your self-worth but also stall your productivity completely by attaching your ability to the failed outcome. The failed outcome can leave you disenchanted from trying again, and that exacerbates the problem. You can end up not trying again, and the whole incident just adds to your glossary of incomplete tasks. Over time, that can accumulate to give you a feeling of worthlessness. Perfectionism can make you feel all of your self-worth depends on what you achieve and that others also judge you by the same criteria (Winfield, 2015).

This overt need for perfection has been linked to procrastination and imposter syndrome, which we will look at in the next chapter. However, it is necessary to note that perfection is a myth. There is never a final say on how something can be done perfectly. Thinking otherwise can be a bit arrogant on our part.

Since we are on the move to shift perspectives, thinking differently about this, too, can be helpful. Imagine perfection as an ongoing continuum having no end. There is no final point to it. Today you can be near perfection, but tomorrow someone else will be. And the day after, someone else. Every subsequent attempt can bring you closer to it, but there will be no finality. So, it is futile to think that elusive perfection is defeat. It is just an opportunity to learn something more.

Myth #5: Your Worth Depends on Your Partner

Having a supportive relationship with a partner can be an enriching experience for many of us. And, since we share our lives with them, our sense of self can get inextricably linked with them. When people grow and evolve together in a relationship, they can create a magical and uplifting environment for each other.

But the opposite of it is true as well. Sometimes, relationships get messy for a number of reasons and turn sour. The most common reason for this misconception, that your worth depends on your partner, is the distorted portrayal of romantic relationships in popular media. These representations are as much skewed as they are patriarchal, favoring a particular kind of hetero-normative dynamic that mainly portrays women in a supportive role in the protagonist's story. Think of all the love stories from the animated Cinderella to modern-day flicks with the damsel in distress narrative. Even traditional family roles and cultural idioms of a woman's worth attached to being a supportive wife set the stage for not only experiencing but aspiring to this relationship dynamic.

Depending on our attachment styles and levels of self-worth, we can either deal with conflicts in a fruitful manner or make the environment completely toxic by tearing each other down. What is supposed to be an exciting experience can leave us anxious.

According to attachment theory, there are four attachment styles, each impacting the quality of relationships we have as adults. There is the anxious attachment style, where a person is always looking for responsiveness and reassurance from their partner because they hold a negative-self-image of themselves and a better view of others. Then there is the avoidant or dismissive attachment style, where a person has high self-esteem and does not rely on emotional closeness from others. Third is the fearful-avoidant attachment style, in which a person is ambiguous regarding emotional closeness as they want to have intimacy but cannot wholly have interpersonal trust. Finally, there is the secure attachment style, where a person is secure within their self-image as well as has a positive outlook on others. Such people are comfortable with emotional intimacy and rely on their partners for support and, in turn, allow the partners to rely on them as well (The Attachment Project, 2023).

People with low self-worth can be trapped in the cycle of seeking constant reassurance from their partners and depend on them for their happiness. Often they can be in codependent relationships where they prioritize the needs of their partners and attach their entire worth to the relationship's success. As we have seen, people with low self-worth have a not-so-good view of themselves and may keep others on a higher pedestal. Since their sense of self is weak, they fear what might happen if their partner leaves them.

But the truth is, no matter how much you hold on to the idea of another person making your life worthy, it is just not the case. A loving and supportive partner can share in your happiness, and you can share in theirs, but no other person can give you your worth. They can love you, but they cannot make you feel positive about yourself beyond a point. And, because this person is perhaps the closest to you in terms of emotional intimacy, it can become extremely difficult to detach your self-image from them and have healthy boundaries.

Your self-worth is an internal concept. It comes from being secure in your own values and personality. And a healthy, loving relationship that celebrates you can only happen when you celebrate yourself.

Discarding Myths: Strategies to Reclaim Your Self-worth

Now that we have seen some major myths surrounding self-worth let's bust them with these strategies.

Taking the Time to Know and Accept Yourself

If you have thought about healing yourself from low self-worth, chances are you have come across this whole idea of getting to know yourself. Philosophers have talked about it, spiritual gurus have sworn by it, and life coaches have emphasized it. When something is said enough times, it gains a tendency to become saturated and lose all meaning. If you have also looked at this section and thought, jeez, not this again, I promise you that this is the soul of self-care.

But what exactly do we mean when we say know yourself? And can we ever honestly know ourselves entirely as we are? While the second question is a mind-bending philosophical question that requires twisty reflection, we can easily answer the first one.

Getting to know yourself or self-discovery is about becoming aware, acknowledging every part of yourself, and owning it up, including your strengths and self-perceived shortcomings. It is about being anchored in yourself. Everything is there within you, the good, bad, ugly, and the gray, but only you have the power to choose what you want to focus on.

And how can you know yourself? Just like you come to know pretty much everything else in life by asking questions. Only here, these questions are directed toward yourself and can be approached from different dimensions. Although a simple-looking process, it does not come with a straight know-it-all manual. But that is an excellent thing. We are fortunate because it gives us a wonderful opportunity to be creative and, more importantly, authentic. *You* can decide the what and how of knowing yourself so that there is a deep sense of safety and calm when you reflect on questions about yourself. We will look at this more closely in the seventh chapter, but it is essential to highlight it here as a crucial step in reclaiming your self-worth.

At this point, we should also make a mental note of two guiding principles in the self-discovery process: *patience* and *acceptance*.

Patience because in our fast world, we look for quick end-all solutions. But knowing yourself is not a journey with a definite end. It is a meandering path, like life, which evolves with you for as long as you're alive. Therefore, thinking about it as a dynamic and continuously transforming process can save you from feeling frustrated about not having clear answers. Whatever answers you find out for yourself are subject to change as you keep growing.

Next is acceptance because accepting ourselves can bring us peace. But wait up, do you think that acceptance is hard precisely because you don't like certain aspects of yourself and would like to change them? You may also wonder if acceptance sounds like an excuse to remain as you are and justify one's poor behavior in many cases. I hear you, dear friend, but I want to draw your attention to a slightly different way of thinking about this.

Acceptance can function on different levels in our lives. Consider the following statements:

- I can *accept* that I didn't prepare well, so I failed a test.

- I can *accept* and grieve the loss of someone dear.

- I can understand that our world is battling climate change, so I need to *accept* my responsibility for being an environmentally conscious user.

Notice the different contexts and implications each of these examples has. In the first instance, accepting is about taking responsibility and facing the consequence of something that has already happened. Regardless of the background reason for not preparing well, I accept that I didn't and understand the result. Acceptance allows me to try again with better preparation. In the second instance, acceptance is about making peace with circumstances that are beyond my control and cannot be changed. In the third instance, acceptance goes a step beyond and becomes something more, like taking positive steps to ensure I don't litter or use recyclable goods as my contribution toward protecting the environment.

As you can see, acceptance is about taking responsibility for actions you can control and making peace with things you cannot control. But above all, acceptance means allowing yourself to make a positive change for yourself and acknowledging yourself for it.

It is the same in the context of knowing yourself. Accepting yourself becomes a tool to detach your sense of self and character from external circumstances. So, when you come to know yourself, you authentically accept yourself for who you are and do not attach your worth to something outside of yourself or someone's opinion of you. Your worth comes from yourself, your values, and whatever makes you a unique human being.

Honest Evaluations but Avoiding Moral Judgments

You know that monologue running in the background that sounds like you, always accompanies you, and seldom remains quiet? Yes, that is the internal dialogue we all have, and it shapes our internal narrative.

When we say that our minds are constantly trying to make sense of our experiences, we don't just mean the various neurological processes inside our brains but also this voice that provides a free-running commentary on the world and ourselves. This voice is crucial for our self-worth, and we can befriend it.

Quite often, this internal monologue is our harshest critic and downright offensive! For people with low self-worth, it puts them down with shame even before the external world has a chance to say something mean. And this makes it harder for them to recover from negative experiences.

Now, reflection is unavoidable, and so is comparison. When we feel we have done something that falls short of the ideal standard, it is natural to judge ourselves in an unfavorable light and pass a quick moral judgment on how we have let down the people around us. But how many times do we really take a moment to counter that judgment? And how many times do we adopt an encouraging and forgiving approach in our self-evaluation? If you are saying never or seldom, then come here, sit down, and listen up.

Giving yourself an honest and open evaluation is very important, but so is the tone in which you do so. When we are very young, our tone may be influenced by the people around us, our family and parents, but as we grow, we start figuring out our voice. Sometimes, it takes a very long time before we know whose voice we are imitating while talking to ourselves. And many times, we never arrive at this question altogether. But even if it is your tone now after years of experiencing life, it is essential to check its quality.

So, the next time your internal monologue is bordering on being vitriolic, stop and take a moment. Hug yourself if that helps, and change your tone toward yourself. Think about the ideal person you needed to look up to as a child and be that person to yourself. Allow yourself to be loved by you and tell yourself that it is okay to make mistakes. It is okay to falter, and it does not make you a bad person but a very normal human being. Ask yourself, how can I avoid making the same mistake, or what steps can I take to solve this problem? Never forget to tell yourself that you've got it because you really have got it. You can do it.

And lastly, honest evaluation includes giving yourself a pat on the back for every win, no matter how small or big. For everything you feel you have messed up, there is a thing you have done right. So, celebrate your wins, feel proud of your achievements, and focus on your positives.

Body Positivity

The way to tackle one of the most dangerous self-worth myths out there is to cultivate a positive body image. What is body positivity all about? It is much more than the presence of trending size-inclusive clothing options available across shopping platforms.

But before getting into what body positivity is, a damaging myth about it must be dispelled. Some people erroneously equate body positivity with being a fad promoting complacency over obesity or nurturing a habit of making excuses for being overweight. This is not only misinformed; it is dangerous, completely distorted, and biased. Our physical frame depends on so many uncontrollable genetic and biological factors that it makes no sense to think about a universal standard. But we all have subjected ourselves to it, whether knowingly or unknowingly, mostly, as a result of years of exposure to images and products that deliberately create a need to look a certain way in order to be considered worthy.

But body positivity has got nothing to do with your weight and *everything* to do with how you feel about yourself in your body, in your own skin. You can weigh xyz pounds above or below some abstract ideal weight standard and feel happy about yourself, or fall within the ideal range and have major body image issues. Body positivity is about recognizing these issues and appreciating all shapes, nonetheless. It aims to break the ideal body type stereotype because there *is* no universal ideal, and there shouldn't be.

Imagine visiting a flower shop and only finding red roses. How boring! Let there be orchids, lilies, poppies, chrysanthemums, daisies, bluebells, asters, and every other kind you can think of. Differences are just differences, not a superior or inferior status chart. Diversity is something to be celebrated and empowered rather than boxed in.

We become so obsessed with our supposed lack of features that we forget to look at the things we do possess. And what we do possess is our body. It is the only one we were born with and destined to live in, and it supports us through so much. Maybe we should start thinking of it as our personal space shuttle that not only carries us around but protects our beautiful selves from the weird toxic radiation of social expectations! And we, in turn, should start appreciating and loving it more.

Body positivity, then, is about taking control of the narrative of loving ourselves through our bodies. It is about moving freely, letting our silhouette create beautiful shapes instead of trying to bend and break in unnatural ways to fit the mold. Here are a few great ways to start loving your body that can help in promoting a healthy self-image:

- Compliment yourself every day using affirmative and empowering words. Take the time to notice something about your body that makes you feel confident.

- Normalize natural things that our bodies do. Yes, that includes normalizing acne and body hair. They are as normal as breathing, and you shouldn't have to change anything unless you want to.

- Appreciate your body's ability to endure stress and still keep going.

- Experiment with your style, not for anyone else but for yourself. If you genuinely want that hairstyle, don't listen to that nosey hairdresser who tells you it won't suit your face or body type.

- Devote time to indulge in movement-based activities that encourage a mind-body connection and foster a sense of comfort. Should you do the crazy dance? Yes, definitely!

- Don't be concerned about your weight for anything other than a choice for happy and healthy living. Think about being active rather than slim/fat.

- Because we cannot avoid comparisons entirely, be mindful and realistic. Instead of an either-or comparison focusing on what they have, and you don't focus on what you both have and appreciate the difference.

Identifying Negative Relationship Patterns and Cultivating Healthy Ones

A toxic relationship, whether romantic or otherwise, can feel like constantly walking on eggshells, worrying about the next problem or having a fear of abandonment. And we have discussed the mutually reinforcing link between negative relationship patterns and low self-worth. How can one break this chain?

Since relationships play a huge role in our lives, identifying healthy ones from unhealthy ones becomes essential in recovering self-worth. Even though the internal dynamics of every relationship are different, you can look for some signs to identify negative patterns in your relationships:

- not feeling heard or supported

- difficulty in voicing your needs due to feelings of guilt and anxiety

- facing verbal, mental and emotional (gaslighting), and physical abuse

- complete codependency in the relationship characterized by one party being the constant provider and the other being a constant receiver

- negative emotions like jealousy and distrust that threaten safety and have the potential to blow up

- inability to freely share opinions or safely express disagreements

- inability to be present for your partner or hyper-emotional independence (yes, sometimes we require self-work too)

- not aligned with your overall values as a person

- inability to resolve conflicts or avoiding communication aimed at resolving problems just to maintain peace (partners not taking the responsibility to grow the relationship)

- inability to set boundaries and making your life revolve around one person

- adopting your partner's likes and dislikes without leaving scope for your individuality

- having a constant need to play the savior and justifying unacceptable behavior

Identifying what works for you and doesn't is not an easy road. Sometimes it takes us to the darkest corners of our mind. It is a process that calls upon us to face our worst fears. But I promise you that this self-work can teach you self-reliance and free you from the burdens that bind so many of us, and keep us from fully enjoying and appreciating friendships or companionships.

So, what steps can you take to build healthy relationships?

Firstly, you have to think of every relationship in your life as a symbiotic connection where you add something to it and gain something from it. Take note of what each relationship adds to your life and then see what you need from it. Only when you become conscious of your needs can you take the steps required to build healthier relationships.

This also means realizing the difference between needs and expectations. Needs being met does not automatically mean that every expectation you have will be or should be held up. As much as it is about other people valuing your space and autonomy, it is about you being able to reciprocate that for them. Sometimes we put unrealistic expectations on others that may not be fair to them. Therefore, the importance of self-work is in finding that balance between being there for people and letting them be there for you.

Having said that, the next step is to start taking note of your feelings around the most significant people in your life. Do they have a calming effect on you or leave you anxious? Do they inspire and support you in your times of need, or do they criticize you for your troubles? This can help you determine the quality of the relationship. While it may not be easy to face the truth of a relationship, it is important to figure out how you want to respond to it.

Then, start noting how people react to you when you tell them about your needs. Do they provide a safe space or at least a sympathetic ear to listen? If they are open to making changes accommodating your needs, you can work on it with them, but if not, you can decide to let go of such people. It is also true that sometimes it may not be possible to cut ties with toxic people, for example, with relatives, but you can take steps to minimize your involvement with them.

We will talk about this and the importance of saying no in more detail in the sixth chapter when we see how to build a strong support system for yourself. The key is to realize that healthy relationships don't make you feel guilty for taking care of yourself.

Letting Go of the Pressure to Be Perfect

Remember Jonathan from the first chapter? He may have continued with the project if he could have sent that demo without obsessively needing it to be perfect.

The perfection madness can manifest in different areas of our lives ranging from personal appearances to professional performance. It actually has the opposite effect on us. Instead of motivating us to do good, the pressure puts us in a loop of criticism and procrastination. Because we want to do our best, we postpone doing something until the absolute last minute, and then the time crunch ends up creating a situation in which we cannot perform our best. The catastrophizing scenario comes true.

It doesn't stop there. The pressure to be perfect seeps into every role that we play. Being the perfect student, parent, friend, employee, and so on.

The narrative for perfection comes from an assumed finality. Meaning we feel that once we have done something perfectly, it is going to be that way for all times to come. But shifting this narrative, shifting what perfection means to you, can help you relieve this pressure. Sometimes perfection is doing whatever you can in a given set of circumstances. It is about showing up when giving up is easier. Remember that everyone deals with a separate set of issues and has different strengths. And, honestly, no matter how extraordinary you train yourself to be, someone will always come along with a different insight or a better way to do something. Perfection then means having the grace to try *your* best and *letting go of the comparison*. If anything, the only valid comparison should be with yourself. In a cumulative sense you can hone yourself to be better than your past self every day. Every time you do something, you get something more that adds to *you*.

So, shift the narrative of perfection. Bring in the importance of quality and meaningfulness. But there is more to it. The worst effect of seeking constant perfection is feeling like an imposter upon failing to do so. The next chapter takes a deep dive into making sense of the imposter syndrome and strategies to deal with it.

Chapter 3:

Understanding Imposter Syndrome

Do you ever wonder what a weird name for this phenomenon of acute self-doubt is? Imposter syndrome! The undertones of this word, imposter, has some uncomfortable vibes attached to it as if the imposter is lying to everyone else and herself too. It is akin to wearing a mask of competence that anyone can peel off if they get too close to you. This feeling of hiding something and thinking you are at fault even when you have done nothing wrong intensifies the feeling of being a fraud. Overcompensating for it in different ways weighs you down.

So, what is this? And why is this? Imposter syndrome is more than your average healthy dose of self-doubt. And it is corrosive to your sense of self at all levels.

Decoding Imposter Syndrome

On a rainy evening with storm warnings, Coco faced an urgent emergency and needed to board a flight to her hometown. She did not have the time to book her tickets, so she arrived at the airport directly from her workplace and made it to the ticket counter. The flight scheduled to leave next had no seats available, and the rest of the flights were canceled due to the storm warning. The man at the counter politely apologized for the inconvenience and told her he could not do anything. She stepped aside and started making a few calls to figure out if there was another way for her to travel that evening. After almost half an hour of fidgeting and pacing around in front of the counter, she heard the man from the ticket counter call her. He informed her that two passengers had canceled their tickets at the last moment, and he could squeeze her in. Relieved at the news, she paid and got her ticket, thanked the man, and quickly proceeded to check-in. She sighed and thanked her luck.

That's luck! Last minute coincidences, her still being present at the right place at the right time! Surely, that was luck.

You must naturally wonder, what has that little story got to do with imposter syndrome? Aren't we supposed to decode and understand that rather than read a story about luck? Yes, and that will become clear in a moment.

Imposter syndrome, or imposter phenomenon at that time, was described in 1978 by Dr. Pauline Clance and Dr. Suzanne Imes in their study concerning female students and professionals, pointing to a condition where successful women failed to internalize the experience of their success. Over time, it is now realized that it is a wider phenomenon affecting many people (Hibberd, 2019).

Imposter syndrome is characterized by a feeling in people that their success and achievements are a result of everything else but their own efforts. That they have somehow managed to fool the system, maybe gotten too lucky, and that their success is illegitimate. Despite demonstrating competent skills, they feel less capable than the credit accorded to them (Braslow et al., 2012).

There is always a strange anxiousness and self-doubt attached to whatever they do, feeling like there is always someone else capable of doing it better. Often seen in high-performing individuals, who would otherwise come across as having nothing to be nervous or insecure about, this intense experience of self-doubt makes them feel like outsiders in their workplace. But imposter syndrome doesn't restrict itself to successful people. It can appear in different people at different stages of life in different contexts. And the anxiety attached to it is very difficult to explain to others, especially if you have achievements that people praise you for. Yet, the common point is that people with imposter syndrome put others with similar skills on a higher pedestal and downplay their own qualities. The biggest lie they tell themselves is that it is all luck and fortune.

Yes, that is a big and powerful lie. And this is where the previously described story comes into play. What Coco faced that day was luck and favorable circumstances, with two passengers canceling their tickets at the last minute. She couldn't do anything to influence their decision, but her luck got her where she needed to be. But do you think this is the case with you? Think about it. You *have* worked for the things you want, and you *have* done something about it, but you have forgotten to take note of those efforts.

Is It So Simple?

The problem sounds simple enough when described as a false belief in one's inability. But the tentacles of this problem go deep. As Dr. Hibber explains in *The Imposter Cure: How to Stop Feeling Like a Fraud and Escape the Mind-Trap of Imposter Syndrome*, people can construct various myths around imposter syndrome, such as it helps them stay humble, keeping them safe and motivating them to work harder and seek perfection. But the truth is that it holds you back and stops you from enjoying your success (Hibberd, 2019).

It is a false safety blanket that puts you in autopilot mode, and sometimes you cling so tightly to your identity as a serial self-doubter that is trying to come out of it can feel like losing a safety net. The difficulty is that you can easily convince yourself of this twisted tale in which believing yourself to not be good enough acts as a crutch to fall back on. If you already begin from a place of compromised ability, you can shield yourself from supposed failures. *Oh, I was never competent enough to begin with; it is only natural that I failed.* But the only thing it ends up doing is adding to that anxiety and creating a bubble of shame and fear.

This is an extremely hard situation to get out of, but not impossible. You must ask yourself to take a hard look at where these feelings come from and try to find out why they exist. If you have had difficult and traumatic life experiences, doing it with a mental health professional, like a therapist, can greatly add to your self-understanding from a place of safety.

Why Do You Feel Like an Imposter?

Human beings evolve through a dialectical process. Internal and external experiences interact and create a synthesis. We are influenced by the world and, in turn, influence it. This means that different versions of you exist in other people's minds on one hand and your own on the other. Now, these images may not always match with what you think of yourself. This is where imposter syndrome can be born. Having low self-worth can widen the gap between other people's perceptions of you and your own, causing you to believe you are an imposter.

Experiences as a Child

You may need to be an archeologist of your life here and dig up your past or sift through the archive of your personal life like a historian. It can be a slow process and sometimes difficult, especially if you have trauma in your past. But sometimes, the really meaningful answers to our fears lie in certain key moments of our childhood.

Children look up to their parents for sustenance as well as emotional support, validation, and a strong sense of security. Our core values are influenced by our earliest interactions with our parents and immediate family. These interactions can be decisive in how we will see ourselves. If our parents have been present and encouraging or uninvolved and abusive, their perception of us gets repeated and reinforced in us through internalization. If children are not valued, they can learn to dismiss their achievements (Hibberd, 2019).

Comparison with others in school or even with siblings at home can be a trigger for feeling like an imposter. If comparison has always ended in putting you down, you can internalize the experience of being inadequate. Suppose comparison has ended in people around you not celebrating your success or primary caregivers being dismissive. In that case you can internalize the need to be absolutely spot-on perfect every time to feel worthy.

While childhood experiences are important, Dr. Hibberd explains that it is not necessary that imposter syndrome is always caused by them. Sometimes, the reasons lie elsewhere.

Insecurities in a Personal and Professional Environment

In competitive environments or times of change, you can feel doubt about newer roles and challenges. As part of growing, getting out of your comfort zone is critical, but this very situation can *aggravate* the feeling of not being worthy enough. In that situation, you put pressure on yourself to be perfect (Hibberd, 2019).

The perfectionism we talked about in the last section of the previous chapter connects here. You can have a very rigid path to achieve what you want, and any detraction or detour can make matters worse for you. How? By either pushing off doing things or doing it all yourself, leading to burnout. We will discuss this in a while, but it is necessary to recognize that insecurities have a huge role to play in the experience of feeling like an imposter.

We all have insecurities. No one is born with absolute confidence unless they are psychopaths. Feeling doubt is a natural thing, as life is uncertain. At any given time, you and I cannot predict the future. We cannot even accurately predict our own feelings one year from today.

In such a *probability-based game of life*, insecurities and doubts are just as natural as sunrise and sunset.

But to an imposter, the probability of failure does not remain just a probability. It takes on the form of a self-fulfilling prophecy that will confirm their self-doubt. And it is so damaging that your entire world can crumble under its pressure. Think, for example, if you feel you are insecure in yourself and always think your partner will realize their worth and abandon you for not being good enough for them, the shadow of this insecurity will damage every moment you spend together. You may even end up living in a false relationship where you project being happy and in love, but in truth, you are just scared and anxious. And that holds you back from fully loving.

It is not enough to realize the lies you tell yourself about being an imposter. It is also important to realize that these lies percolate in the deepest areas of your life and leave everything devoid of meaning.

Confirmation Bias of Interpreting Feelings and Beliefs as Facts

Jake and Nora were huge fans of tennis. Nora told Jake how watching every match with butter popcorn reminded her of watching the game with her dad. She swore her father would make her wear white socks every time their favorite players played, as he believed it somehow got them points. And she witnessed it a few times, so she almost believed it too. Jake laughed it off and teased her for this superstition. He asked her to wear the white socks now and see for herself. Funnily enough, she jumped up from the sofa and disappeared into the bedroom, coming out wearing white socks after a couple of minutes. The moment she sat on the sofa, her player got a point. Sure enough, this continued for a while. She turned to Jake with a look of a winner and went, "I told you so."

Do you think it was really white socks? Think before you answer. It is a particularly interesting question. And obviously, there is no straight answer to it. If one believes it honestly was the miracle of the white socks, one is discounting the skill of the player completely and ascribing influence on an object miles away. But let's humor ourselves a little bit. If this is true and everyone comes to know of this magical effect and starts wearing white socks to help their favorite players win, won't it become a fight of the white socks? Which white socks will actually win and have the most influence? Will they also endow players with the ability to have superplayer abilities?

As you keep going down this rabbit hole, you realize how absurd it sounds. Humans are wired to have a brain that keeps a catalog of experiences to access as shortcuts in times of need. These shortcuts can create a confirmation bias as we find familiar patterns in new information and experiences. We are naturally predisposed to look for similarities confirming our pre-existing knowledge of something. Such knowledge may or may not be verified as fact.

Confirmation bias can function internally as well. When we believe in our worthlessness and feel lacking in ourselves, even successful outcomes are not enough to make us see the positives. We get stuck in the process of concentrating on the negative. You made beautiful art, but you will focus on those three imperfect brush strokes. You got the promotion, but you will focus on the fear of challenges instead of your ability to learn.

You can do well, but that is never good enough because your goalpost keeps shifting further and higher away, setting you up to feel you will never reach it. You get the gist!

It is key to actively and purposefully refute such confirmation biases and move toward a self-evaluation that is not criticism heavy.

Socio-Structural Factors and Gender Roles

By now, we have established many times that humans live in communities, and interactions between different communities produce extended communities. You are not just born into your family but a social structure that is characterized by diversity of every kind. Think of how you are part of your local groups, cultures, religious community, region, nationalities, and so on. We also know that this world of extended communities is not an equal one, and people belonging to certain groups may face historical disadvantages such as racial discrimination, gender-based biases, or even difficulties in accessing resources of our society based on physical and mental disabilities.

These structural inequalities also play a foundational role in deciding how confident and valued we feel. Studies spanning the disciplines of psychology, sociology, economics and politics, history, and so on have shown that tradition and modernity intersect a person's life to produce a set of conditions where we get to flow with relative ease and, privilege or we have to fight to make space for ourselves.

Our workplaces are also a microcosm reflecting societal diversity and inequality. They can function with stereotypical assumptions of who is considered competent. One such glaring stereotype pertains to gender roles.

A patriarchal society functions on the basis of traditional roles ascribed to men and women and systematically excludes sexual minorities, homosexuals, and trans persons. Not only that, but it also favors a particular kind of essentialized masculine image of success and competence. If you are a woman, you must surely have your own experiences to vouch for this feeling of being an outsider or not belonging in different areas of your life outside of the narrowly defined confines of family responsibilities.

When people of color enter white spaces, they can feel the pressure to earn their place even when they have actually earned the job or position they are working in. When women enter areas dominated by men, they can feel the additional pressure of proving their acumen and tenacity by working in highly competitive and individualized environments that call upon them to prioritize work over family. In fact, the responsibility to run a family is almost exclusively reserved for women in relationships where both men and women work. And on the other hand, this responsibility is seen as a hindrance which further plays a role in not selecting women for higher positions.

Tulshyan and Burey (2021) explain in detail how self-doubt is aggravated because of such exclusions and biases. This feeling of an imposter, an outsider, then doesn't just exist in people's minds but manifests in reality because of structural factors. Because our workplaces are built in ways that preclude systems of support, we can end up feeling not competent enough.

But in this very predicament, it becomes crucial to interrogate this feeling of self-doubt. Are you feeling inadequate because you are indeed inadequate or because the system is constructed in such a way that it hinders you? Does the way this world functions make you falsely believe that you don't belong? Such studies and stories open you up to a completely different way of looking at imposter syndrome by anchoring it in our social experiences.

Whatever your social position, *you are not the imposter* for not fitting into boxes made for someone else. Instead, you have been wrongly made to feel that way. And it is time to let go of that false belief now.

The Two Poles of Imposter Syndrome: Burnout and Procrastination

The pendulum of imposter syndrome swings between overworking and not working at all. Both of these extremes can be understood in terms of a loop leading to different work styles but always having the same effect: intensifying your feeling of self-doubt.

On the one hand, lies the fear-fueled *burnout loop* of imposter syndrome. Because you are afraid of failing and you deal with perfectionism, you set a high standard of achievement. Since your ideal standard is too high and often unrealistic, it becomes important for you to work exceptionally hard. How else will you satisfy the need to be perfect? Do you see where it goes from here? You're right, you begin working under extreme pressure, and all that hard work further sets the standard for similar hard work for the next time. Welcome to your inescapable trap. You have now entered a vortex of stretching yourself thin so that you maintain this streak lest the ball drops.

Once you complete a task, the cycle resumes. For a secure and confident person, completion signals a period of rest, taking a break, and rejuvenation. But not for you. You consistently put yourself through all of it again because you are struggling with the feeling of fear. If you rest, you will feel guilty and ashamed. So, you don't even take a moment to appreciate your herculean effort. At this point, I just want you to ask yourself, hey, awesome human, why do you do this to yourself? Why are you your own enemy?

This extreme work style not only affects your mental and physical health because, hello, your body is bearing all that strain, but it also has consequences for those around you. Because you attach your worth to the perfect outcome, you can become controlling and micromanage everything. See, imposter syndrome does not function alone. A host of other concerns can come together. In this case, the inability to delegate and trust other people is determined by your belief that if you want something best, you need to do it yourself. My dearest friend, this is a sure-shot ticket to burnout land.

On the other hand, lies another loop—the *loop of procrastination* and putting things off for later. Here the pressure to be the best can take two directions. Either you can just give up and not try anything new that challenges you unless you are sure you can get it right on the first attempt. Or, if you cannot avoid the task, you leave it to the last moment to avoid uncomfortable thoughts associated with self-doubt. These unpleasant thoughts function like a pre-formed judgment about yourself as not being capable. So, by procrastinating, you just delay arriving at that pre-formed judgment. Fear of failure converts into a belief that you necessarily will fail. And, when you do get to work after you can no longer procrastinate, you again set yourself up for extreme pressure.

This second loop also has related consequences like avoiding difficult situations, not asking for help to avoid feeling vulnerable, self-sabotage, and indifference. In extreme situations, people can reach a stage of self-destruction and become prone to unhealthy addictions to cope (Hibberd, 2019).

Both poles of imposter syndrome, burnout, and procrastination, are unhelpful.

Accessing the Truth by Reversing the Narrative

When we tell ourselves a few lies repeatedly and practically live with them, they become our deeply held truths. But if they are false, as we have seen in the previous sections, we can allow ourselves to adopt better beliefs and truths that fulfill us. So, I would like your permission to show you how to access newer truths by reversing the narrative of imposter syndrome. The following pointers can help you in thinking differently about yourself:

- You are not born with all the capabilities, but you can practice.

- You can seek out evidence in your support.

- You can ask yourself if you hold everyone to the same standard of perfection as yourself.

- You can be afraid of something and still do it.

- You can reverse the negative mental map to code in your positive efforts.

Let's start here with the first pointer: even if you are not proficient enough at the moment, is anything stopping you from doing the work that will make you good enough? The only person stopping you is you. The point is to cut yourself some slack and begin the work on yourself. It is perfectly alright to feel self-doubt, but realizing that you can minimize it is equally important. If the milk or some other staple runs out in your home, I am sure you don't convince yourself that you are never going to have it ever again! No, you make your grocery run and get the thing you ran out of. Similarly, even if there is something you are not skilled enough at the moment, you can practice becoming adept at it, no?

Seek out the evidence in your support. Dr. Hibberd explains this strategy quite fruitfully. How is it possible that anything that goes wrong is entirely your fault, but anything that is good is not your excellence but luck? Make a list of your achievements, no matter how big or small, and take note of all the efforts you have put in. Take the time to reflect on it comprehensively. Don't get stuck on secondary reasons for how it happened. The key is to realize that your evidence for your incapability only relies on your thinking and not actual facts. By making a list like this, you get factual proof of your accomplishments. *You* have achieved all that by your hard work and not anyone else. And you can rely on it every time the spiral of self-doubt threatens your peace of mind.

Talking to friends and colleagues about such experiences can also help you in gaining a different perspective on your skills as well as an insight into how common the experience of self-doubt is. Even the people you may think are terrific at their jobs will tell you about their moments of weakness.

Next, you can contemplatively ask if the standard of insane perfection you hold dear is applicable to everyone or just you. Chances are you downplay yourself and think of others as already perfect. If you offer support to a friend and ask them not to put themselves through so much pain, you can turn this kindness inwards. Everyone has a different threshold of perfection anyway, so there is no one perfect way that fits all.

Moving on, think of growth. If something you really want to do makes you feel afraid, all the more reason to do it. We spend so much time denying ourselves the opportunity to honor all aspects of our personalities. As children, we are more open to silly joys and trying out anything that gives us a sense of exhilaration. Growing up, we become concerned with how others will see us. But inside, the child is perhaps still yearning for that freedom. And if there is anything you owe to anyone, it is this inner child. I promise you that the satisfaction of trying out will be unparalleled, and it can give a boost to your confidence. Remember, it does not matter whether you get things right in the first go, but it matters that you try. Life is a collection of such experiences, which become thrilling chapters in your story. Allow your character development!

Lastly, take baby steps and code them all in your memory. Make an inventory you can access every time you do something new. Note down your fears and emotions associated with the problems you face and every little milestone you cross in solving those problems. Keep doing it so you have enough experiences to count on whenever you're in doubt. This way, you can replace your negative past experiences with positive experiences making a mental map you can rely on. It can be your personal mirror that shows you how far you have come, and like every time, you can keep going. Trust your ability to learn. You learned how to walk, speak, or do basic things to exist! You can learn this too.

It is vital to see that constantly responding to fear sucks out any joy whatsoever from whatever you do. Even if you end up making your passion into a career, the imposter syndrome will render it meaningless as you alienate yourself more and more from the love involved in creating something. All these strategies can guide you in breaking the hold of imposter syndrome, but none of it will work if you don't meaningfully challenge the most formidable enemy: negative self-talk. This is what we turn to next.

Chapter 4:

Challenging Negative Self-Talk

Let's do a thought experiment here. You will need a pen/pencil and paper or anything you can type on.

Imagine you have a close friend named Jane. Jane is participating in the Olympics as a badminton player representing your country. She has managed to reach the finals and is hopeful of reaching the finish line with a gold medal around her neck to bring home. Her match is scheduled for the evening, and she still has some hours before she goes all in. She is understandably anxious because she is facing the same opponent she lost to a few years ago. She decides to take a few moments and call you. During the conversation, she brings up how she can almost feel the medal slipping out of her grasp as her opponent is perfectly prepared, and they have a history there. Her anxiety almost reaches you through the telephone. She says she is confident, but as the time of the match is approaching, she can feel her confidence chip away. With a resigned tone, she says, "Anyway, it wouldn't be anything new if I lose again. After all, I always slip up at the last moment like a loser". You immediately stop her and say, "Jane…"

Now, I want you to stop here and write your response. Write or type what you will say to Jane and then come back.

I will give you two sample replies below and then you can see which one is closer to your response.

First, "Jane, I told you so many times that you should have pushed yourself more. We both know you don't make full use of smash shots to shut out your opponents. And your saves for a close net shot are quite poor. Your opponent knows this and will use it to her full advantage. Your history is only going to help her in utilizing your weak spots. But think clearly and don't let her get to you. All the best. You've got to kill it, babe."

Second, "Jane, deep breaths! You're right that there is history between you two, but you have grown since your last face-off. I have seen you work so hard, and you're as sharp as anybody else on that court. You have continuously practiced your game, and you have got to believe in yourself today. You have defeated so many brilliant players to get here. One person is not going to take that away from you. You're the best. Just use your heart and mind, and you will bring it home. All the best, babe. You got this!"

Notice that the first response brings up negative past experiences in a crisis situation that Jane is already worried about. Even though it ends with all the best, it has an undertone of blame. The "I told you so" many times appears to be not very kind.

But the second response is different. It also uses the negative past experience but adds positivity to it in order to encourage Jane to have faith in her practice. It also highlights how much she has achieved by simply reaching this point. Doesn't it look more encouraging?

Whatever your response may have been, I am sure you have used inspirational words as well. Now, think of similar situations when you felt an absolute terror of not living up to some expectation. How did you encourage yourself? Did you become your most ardent supporter? Did you show yourself kindness? If yes, great, but if no, then you need to start doing this now.

Part of your healing journey is recognizing all the ways you have talked yourself down and making positive efforts to change that. Remember that how you talk to yourself goes a long way in deciding how you feel about yourself. Let's explore the forms negative self-talk can take.

What Can Negative Self-Talk Sound Like?

Talking negatively to yourself is more than just internally saying negative words. It can take different forms that reinforce a negative self-image. It can also mean putting yourself down in front of others. It can also mean a hateful expression you give yourself while looking in the mirror. Or curtailing your wardrobe choices, thinking that particular thing won't look attractive on your body type. And sometimes, it seems like an innocuous passing remark about yourself, but it has dangerous consequences for your self-worth. Mayo Clinic (2022) lists some common forms of negative self-talk:

- *filtering* and *magnifying*, where you blow negative aspects of yourself out of proportion and filter out the positives

- *personalizing* and *catastrophizing*, where you take the blame automatically if something goes wrong and you are always preoccupied with worse-case scenarios

- *polarizing*, where the outcomes are always either good or bad with no mitigating middle ground

Here are some common but by no means exhaustive examples of negative self-talk:

- I am doomed to be this way and will never change.

- I am a dodo, dumbo, or similar name-calling.

- I can never do anything right.

- If people really knew me, they would see the darkness within me and abandon me.

- I am so stupid that I can't learn from feedback.

- I am not deserving of love and support.

- No one actually likes me; they're just polite.

- I am a loser who only makes excuses instead of putting in the effort.

- I am just lazy.

- I am cursed somehow and end up spoiling whatever I touch.

- The universe must hate me. That is why I am not talented enough.

- I can't ask for help, or people will know that I am a fool.

- I am not interesting at all, not intelligent, just average.

- I always let people down.

- I don't really care about anything, and indifference protects me.

- I am incapable of understanding and working on complex stuff.

- I should always steer clear of responsibilities because I can't handle them.

- No one would want me on their team.

- I will always find a way to mess up my happiness.

- I should just give up before making a fool out of myself.

- I can't carry that style; I am not stylish enough.

- My face is gross and ugly.

- I should keep my mouth shut because my thoughts and opinions don't seem to matter.

- My time has gone, and now I can never get it back.

- My needs are not a priority.

- I am just a crybaby with tantrums.

- I absolutely hate myself for lacking xyz (it could be anything).

- I don't have the power to change my life, so I better accept and compromise.

- Everybody will laugh at me if I do this.

- My parents, children, partner, colleagues, and everyone else hate me.

- Agreeing with someone who says mean things about you.

- Using self-depreciation as a coping strategy and feeling like you are not worth having self-respect so people can walk over you.

Anything that begins with I can't, or I lack, that stops you from having faith in yourself and your abilities is a form of negative self-talk.

You may think that you have been living with this pattern for so long that it's a part of your DNA. You might have even tried to free yourself from it with unsuccessful attempts. You may wonder if you can positively get rid of it. I want to tell you that you absolutely can. *You can.*

Strategies to Challenge Negative Self-Talk

Challenging and rectifying negative self-talk revolves around gently nudging yourself away from severely critical ways of thinking about yourself and devising everyday coping strategies that can be utilized to shift the focus to one's strengths and build greater confidence.

Identifying Triggers and Externalizing Fears

All of us have a constant background inner talk going on most of the time about the most mundane activities like remembering daily tasks to be completed, choices and decisions about daily routines, meals of the day, and so on. But there is always something immediate that triggers anxious negative self-talk. These triggers can be:

- existing stress about something you are preoccupied with

- an urgency related to a task, such as deadlines

- inability to avoid a conflictual environment in personal and professional settings

- pressure to perform a certain way (perfectionism)

- anxieties and insecurities connected to past memories of failure

- behavior and responses of other people

Identifying that immediate trigger can help in charting a pathway of thoughts. The why of things is always of utmost importance. Here is how you can try this.

When you find yourself anxiously worrying over something and stuck in the loop of negative criticism, take a moment to reflect on your thoughts at that very moment, the what of the situation. Note down your fears as clearly as possible. Be elaborative and descriptive. Also, take stock of why you are feeling this. Describe in detail what you think will happen if you do or don't do something, the outcome.

Externalizing feelings in this way can help you gain some control over them and understand your unique thought pathways. What I mean by this is that you can identify the process and connection between triggers and negative spirals by writing them out there. Once you know how your thoughts react to certain situations, you can detach yourself from those negative thought patterns. This differentiation is important to make you realize that you are not your thoughts.

The next step would be to use the technique of seeking evidence in the previous chapter. An assessment of the situation can give you an insight into knowing whether your fears are really standing on a solid foundation or not. Talking and sharing your experience with others can be further helpful in discerning the truth. From here, you can gently shift your perspective toward taking control of the situation. This is a shift from *oh no, I can't* to *I can, I'll be okay.*

Checking Negative Emotions by Cultivating Positive Ones

Dr. Julie Smith in Why Has Nobody Told Me This Before? charts out an effective way of checking your emotions. Exploring your emotions is an enlightening activity. Sometimes you can feel things that are impossible to categorize under one label. She advises readers to use as many labels and terms as possible to describe their emotional states and keep track of them through journaling. She also advises people to try seeking new playful experiences like reading a new book, trying new meals, traveling to different places, and meeting new people. Making a note of the feelings associated with them is like collecting and building up an arsenal of positive experiences. Consistently doing this can help in deliberately cultivating certain feelings. This, in turn, strengthens the neural pathways associated with feeling positive (Smith, 2022).

The point is to have enough rewarding experiences backed up in your mental hard drive that anytime you struggle with worthlessness, you can call upon them to counteract that feeling. It can help you sail through with relatively less difficulty.

Purposeful and Constructive Self-Talk

By now, you have a fair idea of how much our internal monologue can affect our actions in the real world. They can either predispose us to take action aimed at success or derail the entire process altogether. When we become mindful of how we talk to ourselves, we open the door to a powerful transformation. Think of it as the most vital problem-solving tool. When we encounter a difficult situation, we assess it and tell ourselves how to get around it. Our brains are equipped with the rational faculties of analyzing a problem and devising ways to solve it. But negative self-talk takes up so much energy that it precludes this faculty of our mind. If you sit back and think about it, the history of human evolution and civilizational leaps point to the fact of how extraordinary we can be. And some of the brightest minds in the world have been regular people like you and me. The important thing is not to shame ourselves for giving in to our self-doubt but to keep moving on despite it.

This is where purposeful and constructive self-talk comes in. Drown out the reductive voice in your head that only acts as a detractor and replace it with an inspiring and encouraging one. For every negative thought, make it a point to counter it with a positive one immediately. Show yourself the possibilities of success and believe that you are just as good as anyone to achieve it.

You may wonder about the possibility that positive self-talk might turn into delusional thinking and overconfidence. But that is not the case. There is a difference between delusional thinking and toxic positivity on one hand and constructive self-talk on the other. Toxic positivity is as harmful as negative thinking because it asks you to deny the reality of what you feel in the moment. The idea is not to pretend to be happy and calm when your internal mental halls are burning. Rather, it is to acknowledge the problematic thoughts and feelings without dwelling on them. The same goes for overconfidence. It stems from gross ignorance and a misleading overestimation of one's abilities under a given set of conditions.

But constructive self-talk does neither of that. It does not plunge you into the other extreme. If anything, it is realistic and practical. When you magnify your problems, constructive self-feedback can ground you in reality and point out different ways in which you can make the best of a given situation.

You can practice constructive self-feedback in a number of ways, such as:

- Instead of worrying about what you cannot do, focus on what you can.

- Instead of deriding yourself for not being perfect, focus on incremental betterment.

- Instead of focusing on your lack of natural talents, focus on the growth trajectory of learning skills.

- In place of feeling ashamed for not being worthy, embrace your flaws and accept them as natural and human.

Positive Affirmations Everyday

Continuing with the tone set in the previous section, positive affirmations can further solidify the positive messages you want to give yourself. They act as daily reminders for your soul to start every day with a positive outlook. Affirmations can be centered around various themes like letting go, fostering belief, or I am affirmations. They can sound like *I release my anger*, *I can do this*, and *I am love and light*, respectively. You can either include them in your daily journal, write them out clearly in colorful, bold fonts, or print them out and stick them on the walls of your room or a vision board or even carry them to your workplace. Whatever works best for you.

There is a huge scope for getting creative in this. The idea is to keep them in a place that's visible throughout the day so you can look at them and reflect upon them at different times of the day. Just as writing out negative thoughts can reveal deeper connections between your fears and self-doubt, writing out positive affirmations can establish new connections between your sense of self and your positive attributes.

If you are not a big fan of fancy stationery and don't want to write and stick papers to your walls, there are many different ways in which you can make use of affirmations. Thanks to the technology we have now, you can access affirmations on podcasts or watch YouTube videos with affirmations and calming background music. There are even choices when it comes to videos that combine guided meditation and positive affirmations. There is no restriction either on when you can access these. Some people prefer to watch or listen to them right in the morning before beginning their routine, and some like to listen to them right before sleeping. Really, the choice is yours. You can even devise your unique way to tailor affirmations.

Are you ready to harness the power of affirmations? Here are some to get you started:

- I promise to show up for myself.

- I release the anxiety patterns and fears that hold me back.

- I am unique, and a miracle manifested.

- With every breath exhaled, I release past hurts (you can practice conscious deep breathing with this).

- I forgive myself and allow myself to step into the world with confidence.

- I am okay today, even if not great, and that is a win.

- I am here and present.

- I am allowed to go through phases of ups and downs without lowering my self-esteem.

- I am open to love and support.

- I have everything I need to initiate change in my life.

- I am/I release…(fill this with anything you want).

Cognitive Behavioral Therapy Based Practices

Cognitive Behavioral Therapy (CBT), is described by the American Psychology Association as a psychological treatment for various mental health issues like anxiety disorders and depression, among others, with a focus on changing negative thinking patterns along with behavioral patterns (APA, 2017).

CBT is an effective tool for managing negative self-talk and helps people channel their thoughts toward constructive outcomes. Jay Fournier from the Center for Cognitive and Behavioral Brain Imaging at Ohio State University explains in an interview with CNN that there is a mitigating factor instead of a direct relationship between external events and our behavior. That mitigating factor is interpretation. How we interpret what happens to and around us determines how we feel (LaMotte, 2021).

CBT shows us that our thoughts and emotions arising out of those interpretations may not be accurate. CBT is most effective with a therapist who can guide you and tailor activities to suit your unique concerns. The most significant benefit of CBT is that an active participatory relationship between you and your therapist equips you to help yourself as you learn new strategies to cope.

Having said that, some CBT-based activities can help you in dealing with your negative self-talk.

Mood and Thought Journal

The most common and effective strategy is to keep a mood and thought journal. Keeping track of how you are feeling can reveal recurring patterns. You can do this in different ways. From simple diary entries that flow in a narrative style to jotting down your thoughts and feelings to more organized tabulated forms. Think of yourself as a research project where you are the researcher as well as the subject of your research. While there are multiple things you can write down, there are four broad things you should be looking for: the time and duration when you feel distressed, the content of distressing thoughts, triggers or immediate events that jumpstart your anxiety, and what you do when you are going through distress (your response or behavior, for example, you could avoid working on something or go to sleep, etc.).

The idea behind this self-research is to have a consistent data set with you to figure out what is leading to uncomfortable feelings and how you are dealing with them. With time, you can feel empowered with this knowledge to take positive steps toward change.

Antecedent Behavior Consequence Functional Analysis for Understanding Negative Self-Talk

The Antecedent Behavior Consequence (ABC) model is another popular strategy to learn about your behavioral patterns. The antecedent means a specific event, thing, person, or anything that triggers a particular feeling or behavior in you. The behavior is, of course, how you behave or act in response to the antecedent and then the consequence of that behavior, the outcome. The analysis is meant to look at what kind of behavior accompanies what kind of situation in your life and whether the outcome is constructive or destructive (Ackerman, 2017).

When it comes to negative self-talk, you can utilize this method to evaluate the contributing factors for negative self-talk. For example, you are trying to fill out an application for a master's course, but the process is overwhelming, and you put it off every day, promising you will start the next day. Every day you end up feeling like you can't do it, and it makes you question whether you should even apply. You start questioning yourself negatively. Can you even get into the course and complete it when you can't even fill out an application?

Here, the stress related to your application process is your antecedent, and procrastination is your behavioral response. The consequence is your feeling of low self-worth. The ABC model can help you clearly see your triggers and start unlearning how you react to those triggers by consciously directing yourself away from harmful behaviors.

Reframing Thoughts

Imagine your thoughts are a book, and your negative thoughts are like very sloppy passages that you want to edit out. There are even sections that can be written better. You are the editor here since *you* hold the key to your narrative. You have the power to reframe them.

Yes, it may not be a very forthcoming strategy for you since you have lived with debilitating self-talk for so long. But consciously changing the content of your self-language can happen. It is possible.

This is known as cognitive restructuring, and the idea is to become conscious of your automatic thoughts. Negative self-talk can become automatic because it's what we have been doing to ourselves for so long. Restructuring allows us to modify the language we use when we address ourselves. The process of seeking evidence that we discussed in the last chapter can be used here. You stop to ask if what you are feeling is valid or based on misunderstandings. Have you looked at all the facts of the matter? Has something really happened to make you feel negative about yourself, or are your negative perceptions exaggerated?

Restructuring demands that you write another story with alternative content and scenarios. So, in place of unhelpful thoughts, you think about alternative ways of thinking! Are you confused?? Don't be. It is a process of teaching yourself how to think anew. So, you focus on the thoughts that can be helpful. For example, instead of giving up in a situation, you ask yourself which way of thinking can help me. You identify that certain ways of thinking hold you back, and as part of this restructuring, you feed yourself those ways of thinking that are actually helpful.

People with low self-worth often struggle with their thoughts, constantly writing a doomsday letter to themselves. If you add rejections and failures to the mix, it becomes a psychological prison. Even if we can control our thoughts and learn to think positively, rejections and failures are uncontrollable dimensions of life that can throw us off our journey. So along with inculcating good thoughts, we must also learn how to build our resilience and deal with rejections in life. They are unfortunate, surely, but they don't have to be attached to our self-worth.

Let's shift the narrative about rejections in the next chapter!

Chapter 5:

Rejection, Resilience, and the Growth Mindset

You delude yourself. Yes. The delusion is that you cannot do it!

Do you remember a time when you had epic dreams for yourself? You probably still do, but you no longer connect with them as intensely as some years ago. Have you found yourself standing at the precipice waiting to fly? You may have returned from there a few times. Whatever your vision for yourself, life may have led you to believe that you can no longer reach your personal zenith anymore. Maybe you have thought to yourself that if you knew exactly how things would pan out and what paths would lead you to the treasure, you would try. If only there were no risks.

Risks are a part of life. Taking risks is easier for the things you love. But life does not come easy. And the things you are passionate about *can* make you have sleepless nights and frustrations. Let's be honest. The fear of failure is terrifying, and the weight is crushing. The question, what if, is ever-present. But isn't that the whole point of it? What if I fail? But what if I succeed?

While we may seek the comfort of knowing what is in store for us before embarking on a new journey, none of us can ever predict the future. This can be incredibly freeing or limiting. It is all about perspective. We can teach ourselves to be hopeful and minimize the voice that only focuses on the negative side of the what if.

If you want to be at peace with yourself while living authentically and meaningfully, you will have to release the urge for mental comfort. You have to stop muting the voice that asks you to take the flight. The little tuggings you feel sometimes, the bursts of colors that show you what your world could look like, feel them. Believe them. Let them guide you in navigating rejections and building resilience.

Navigating Rejections Through a Growth Mindset

Rejections are hard but unavoidable. Trying to avoid them altogether restricts us and shifts our focus on constantly running in a crisis mode. Because self-doubt always makes us assume we will fail, we function with a heightened sense of insecurity, and that may actually cause more harm than good. Besides, we have to face the good, the bad, and everything in between. But it doesn't mean we have to live in that shadow of fear either. You have to realize that rejections are not a finality. And they don't mean you will always fail.

There is a way to think constructively about failures. If we shift our mindset about them, we can see that they can be blessings in disguise.

Nurturing a Growth Mindset

In *Mindset: The New Psychology of Success*, Carol Dweck explains the two mindsets that impact our perception of problems and their solutions. These are the fixed and growth mindsets. People with a fixed mindset operate on the principle of innate abilities and tendencies that they think are unchangeable. They often avoid taking action to get themselves out of a crisis because they believe they cannot do anything about it. They believe things cannot change.

People with a growth mindset, on the other hand, do the opposite of this. They believe that abilities are a result of practice and consistency; they're learnable. They look at problems to find a way to fix them or reverse them. For them, a bad experience or an instance of rejection is not irreversible. They don't spend that much time worrying over proving their worth. Instead, the motivating factor for them is learning and getting better (Dweck, 2006).

Everybody fails at some point in their lives. But what transforms ordinary people into extraordinary trailblazers and leaders is the relentless pursuit of their dreams backed by a growth mindset. One of the most successful authors of our times and the creator of the Harry Potter series, J.K. Rowling went through a bunch of rejections before making it. If you go online, you can find so many examples of people who battled failure to emerge on top. From Thomas Edison to Marie Curie to Steve Jobs to Walt Disney to Oprah Winfrey to Hellen Keller and so many other geniuses have fought challenging uphill battles.

These successful people are humans like you and me, with fears and doubts. They don't have some secret ingredient or a magic wand to solve their problems for them. They have learned from their rejections and have continued on. You can give yourself a million reasons to give up, but there is only one reason to go on: the possibility of making your dreams come true. And this possibility is good enough to keep doing the work.

Nurturing a growth mindset is like training your brain to be consistent. It shifts your perspective to view challenges and failures as opportunities to grow and be better. Just like an athlete trains every day, nurturing a growth mindset is like mental strength training. It offers a possible solution to our habits of underestimating ourselves by stressing the importance of orientation. If we are oriented toward learning, we can be open to the possibility of change. All the difference lies here.

Suppose you want to learn to drive but have a fixed mindset. After the first few tries, you would give up, thinking you are not meant to learn to drive or that you are not smart enough to understand the judgments involved in distance, speed, and situational awareness. The problem with a fixed mindset is that it can quickly lead you to underestimate your abilities. But a person with a growth mindset will view the whole situation differently. For them, the point is to get results in increments. Every day spent practicing makes you slightly better than yesterday. That's growth!

Let's nurture a growth mindset!

Redefining Failure, Befriending Challenges

You are not perfect, you are here to learn, and learning can never happen without mistakes. First, you have to accept yourself completely and then think about changing anything at all. Failure does not mean an absence of abilities. Ability means knowing how things are done but also how they are *not* done. Mistakes are just a way to teach you about the latter! Embrace them, and let them guide you to a better path.

As for challenges, you may never know how far you can go if you don't challenge yourself. Think of them not as hurdles only but as milestones. Every challenge is supposed to show you a possible problem that *you* can get around.

Prioritizing Improvements Over Final Judgments

Judgments make you defensive and inflexible, but a will to improve opens you up to vulnerability and asks you to embrace it. There is a reason we use the word *living* to describe the fact of being alive. The -ing shows a condition of continuous doing or being. We are liv*ing*, and we are already doing it for better or for worse. Judgments imply finality, but improvements suggest movement. But nothing's final till you make it final by giving up. Letting your guard down allows you to be flexible and receptive to improvements. This is a more accurate way of seeing yourself: art in the making, work in progress!

Rethinking Success as Continuous Learning

Do you ever wonder what monks do when they concentrate or meditate for hours? Doesn't it look like they're not doing anything? But they will tell you that it's *not* nothing. Even when you feel like you are achieving nothing successful, you are achieving something. Dweck offers a particularly useful insight here. There is a difference between defining success as an outcome or a process (Dweck, 2006).

A fixed mindset stuck on maintaining a persona of perfection will not do anything new that jeopardizes their image. This can mean they will pass up any opportunity to upgrade their skills in a certain area as that would mean they lack something. In the long run, it robs them of a chance to stay fresh and updated, ultimately affecting the achievement of outcomes.

By contrast, someone with a growth mindset thinking of success as a process, can do everything along the way that endows them with newer knowledge. Success here is not fixed but dynamic and evolving. It is synonymous with long-term learning. It also shatters the myth of perfection by showing there is always scope for improvement.

Today's Scores Are Not Tomorrow's Prediction

Scores and markers are not final indicators of our performance and potential forever. Rejection can make us feel like all doors are closed permanently. Alternatively, doing your best can become a habit and an expectation of doing well always. This is simply not true. Whether good or bad, no performance, no outcome is final, and this is more important to realize, especially when dealing with rejection. Nothing can measure your abilities for the future permanently because your abilities are not static. They grow just like you, and you can choose to grow them consciously. Similarly, potential can grow with every milestone. The more you learn, the more you grow and stretch your potential.

Removing the Idea of an Effortless Success

There is no such thing as an effortless success. A brilliant pianist can make their instrument sound like a smooth-flowing river, effortlessly guiding their fingers over the keys. When we see geniuses doing their genius stuff, we only see a partial picture that is presented to us. We often don't have access to the background. But only they know the sweat and tears behind that projection of effortless performance. Positive thoughts and constructive strategies are the food your brain needs in order to get out of its own limiting beliefs. They can keep you going when the going gets tough and help you dismantle the idea that you can get anything with minimal effort. It can aid your willpower by providing a steady dose of drive. You can make use of strategies described in previous chapters to help you in making your efforts sustained during periods of slowdowns.

But Growth Also Doesn't Mean Running With No Rest

Remember the perfectionist burnout we talked about in the third chapter? You have to see the big picture to deal with burnout. You have to ask what ultimately matters to you, or as Mark Manson says in *The Subtle Art of Not Giving a Fuck*, what do you actually give a fuck about? Go all in for things that deeply matter to you but don't get stuck in a cycle to always present yourself as perfect in everything everywhere (Manson, 2016).

Sometimes people can be caught up in a cycle of giving it their all and then feeling completely defeated by rejection. A growth mindset teaches you to get back up and be relentless, yes, but it doesn't ask you to mindlessly beat your head on the wall. It is about resting and taking stock of mistakes mindfully while tweaking things aimed at improving your performance.

Try Even if You're Not Convinced

If you are a seasoned cynic, someone with a lot of experience with things not going as you want them to, you can feel it really difficult to convince yourself for yet another attempt at change. Maybe you have tried some strategies before, and they have not worked for you. The aftermath of rejections can convince you to let it go and accept your case as predestined. But that is exactly where it becomes even more important to trust the process.

No one can guarantee the number of efforts you have to make in order to finally achieve what you want. But with a growth mindset, this is a risk you can take because you will not be preoccupied with a particular outcome but with the learning curve. So even if you are not where you want to be, you are somewhere.

You can set up your own mechanics to work through rejections. Some key actionable takeaways of a growth mindset are:

- Making achievable goals with concrete steps.

- Dividing goals into short-term everyday routine and long-term strategies.

- Keeping track of progress without judgment and committing to improvement every day.

- Don't stop at only keeping track, but actively follow through by taking accountability (trust me, it will be like the holy grail).

- But also, be mindful not to make things so rigid that you end up beating yourself for slipping up. Slip-ups are natural, and the focus should be on resuming instead of stopping.

- Make yourself a personal inventory to note at least one thing you learned that day. Anything goes. Doesn't matter how small or insignificant.

- Be conscious of the balance between working and resting. Too much of a good thing is detrimental!

- Trusting and reaching out to people with similar experiences to learn from them.

- Lastly, a mindset change is not a quick fix but a lifestyle change for your brain. Embrace it like a permanent feature of your life.

After all is said and done, the postscript of a growth mindset tells you to build a growth mindset *with a growth mindset*! One of the pitfalls for people using self-help strategies is that they use it as a temporary mechanism, thinking once they're out of this pickle, they can just go back to how they were. But having a growth mindset is not a final destination that will erase all your earlier patterns. As Dweck points out, we all have a combination of fixed and growth mindsets pertaining to different areas of our lives (Dweck, 2006). The idea is to keep building toward growth so that when we do feel the urge to rely on our fixed mindset, we push through and persevere.

The Road to Resilience

Up until now, we have been shifting the narrative in a particular direction, but I am amazed by how some shifts can be completely counterintuitive yet bang on!

You are ordinary, but so what? That means you can be extraordinary. What? Wait a second; hear me out.

If you are already there and super-fantastic, one slip-up, and everything can go. But if you're never really there, you can continue on a path that is always reaching there. Thinking like this is radically freeing. You free yourself from the pressure to always uphold the label of extraordinary. You can relax and tell yourself that in being ordinary and growth-oriented, I am extraordinary!

This is how you can build resilience because resilience is the resolve to get back up every time you fall. Our talk about improving self-worth is not to establish superiority or inferiority but resilience. It is about being comfortable in your own skin and believing you are amazing because you show up. In a way, the growth mindset is a precursor to a strong, resilient self.

Think of it like this: if you are afraid to fail, maybe you are really afraid of not knowing how to recover from a failure. Maybe you have not put yourself in enough situations that have tested your ability to bounce back from rejections. Perhaps you fear this uncertainty because you don't know if you are resilient enough! Is this a solvable problem? Yes! The more you fail, the more chances you get to build up your resilience. It is up to you to take them. In case you do take them, you will see how a feedback loop is created where the more resilient you become, the more this fear of failure eases, and the more trust you build in yourself.

The growth mindset can endow you with the necessary perspective to foster resilience, and all the strategies we have talked about, move in that direction. But building resilience goes beyond mindset change. It also includes taking steps to build a system that gets activated when you are feeling low on motivation. It involves identifying the things that give you hope and connect with you deeply. To take some examples, these steps can be:

- Looking up to figures that inspire you, and reading about them as well as their stories of triumph.

- Meeting your fears head-on and telling yourself they don't control you.

- Engage in physical movement that gets energy flowing. It doesn't have to be an exercise routine. It can be anything, like dancing or just moving around from one room to another or even from one corner to another.

- Going through your journal/inventory of learnings and achievements or even reading some of your affirmations aloud.

- Using strategies to shut out negative self-talk and check imposter syndrome.

- Reminding yourself of what drives you and the thrill of your dreams, and purposes that give meaning to us are excellent incentives to keep going.

- Developing a strong support system to rely on (this is a particularly valuable one that we will discuss in the next chapter).

I want to leave you with this message here: sometimes, it is imperative to do what you believe in, even when no one else will. Only you have the power over your thoughts and feelings and the capacity to change your mind.

Let's grow resilient now!

Chapter 6:

Developing a Strong Support System

If everyone helps to hold up the sky, then one person does not become tired. –Askhari Johnson Hodari

We began our journey by understanding how interaction between people influences behavior. The internal and external worlds collaborate and collide at different times, having far-reaching effects on our self-image. The first two chapters especially paid attention to the role played by opinions and judgments of people on how we perceive ourselves.

In this chapter, we will flip the story to see that the right people, those who support and uplift us, can energize our souls. We can know all the best things to say to ourselves, but sometimes, we just need to hear it from someone that cares. Support systems act as a network of connected and invested individuals that not only share in our difficulties but also keep us on track by ensuring accountability. Valerie's story can help us understand just how crucial support systems are.

The Victory

Valerie was a 19-year-old athlete with impressive running abilities and track records. She was passionate, committed, and always trying to better herself by never missing her practice session. That fateful day was no different. It had been raining, and her practice stadium was closed. But like a true warrior, she decided to hit the streets. All was good until something happened that would send her on a journey of loss, grief, and triumph.

As she pushed herself to run faster, the wet path affected her shoe grip, and she slipped just as she was coming up to an intersection. What followed was a terrible accident that left her with a fracture of her left leg and injuries to her spine. For the foreseeable future, running was impossible. And there was a strong chance that even after recovery, she may not regain full function in her injured leg.

At first, she was hopeful. *It's just an injury.* It would heal. Within a few months of dedicated physiotherapy, she started walking without support, but it was clear the damage was permanent. The unthinkable had happened. And this broke her heart.

Valerie was being sucked into a black hole internally. On the outside, she looked composed and like someone who had accepted the inevitable. But inside her mind it was a different story. She became withdrawn, irritable, and depressed. And she didn't want to ask for help because she didn't see how she *could* be helped. The grief had taken over completely, and now the blame began. Her friends started seeing less of her, and the ones that did see her walked on eggshells around her, not knowing what would make her angry. It seemed that anything positive in the world or anyone who was happy only reminded her of how broken she was.

She blamed herself for being irresponsible. She was stupid enough to bring this upon herself; it was all her fault. Why did she go out to run that particular day in the rain? And on the streets, no less.

From blame came anger: at herself and the world. Any news of a sporting event, especially a race, triggered her; and she tried to numb the pain. Before she knew it, she was down the rabbit hole of addictions and a heavy dependence on alcohol. Her sense of self took a hit. Who was she, if not an athlete?

The Turn Around

One afternoon, her best friend Mark dropped by her home unannounced. They'd been friends since they were little kids, and he had been there for her through difficult times. He saw that her pain was not only hurting her but everyone around her who loved her.

It was time for a heart-to-heart. After hearing everything Valerie had to say, Mark began.

"Right now is a critical moment where you get to choose who you want to be. If running was your identity, you made it so. Only you can know if you want it to remain so. It will not be easy, but you've got to allow yourself to accept what happened. If it matters so much to you, find a way to still be connected to the sport you love. You're a sportsperson, right? Show me. Acknowledge your circumstances right now and use your sportsman spirit to get out of this bind. Show me how you will not let this be the end of you."

Valerie was partly annoyed but partly surprised at his matter-of-fact tone that was not coddling her. These words swirled in her mind: *you get to choose, find a way to still be connected*. At first, there was resistance, but she listened to that what-if inside her. That night she stayed up researching different support groups. She found one and decided to pay a visit.

Seeing people, sportspersons like her sharing their stories and finding peace, was beginning to motivate her. She shared the unfairness of it all and felt welcomed when people, who knew exactly what she had been through, showed her that *once an athlete, always an athlete*. She got the reassurance that just because she was no longer on the track didn't mean she had lost her identity. Her skill and achievements weren't invalidated. Something changed in her that day.

She reached out to her friends and family one by one, slowly opening up to them, asking them for what she needed: sometimes a sounding board for her to vent, sometimes a friend to offer her encouraging words. They all showed up for her in different ways. For the first time in a long time, she felt open enough to accept the love that poured in for her and realized these people were giving her strength. Relying on them was not a weakness but rather a brave thing to do because it demands that you quiet the ego and be vulnerable. It asks you to accept your humanity!

Between her friends and family, and her support group, there were still moments of sadness and anger for her, but she felt the safety of being supported. She knew that even when some days were going to be hard, her support system would have her back. And, she will have theirs. In being part of the community, especially supporting others, she felt a part of something bigger.

The Return to the Track

Valerie began to dream again and brainstormed with Mark about the possibility of teaching her skills to young budding athletes and people who loved to run and wanted to improve their form. She thought of starting her own coaching practice. She shared these ideas with her support group and received encouragement from them. One of the members shared with her the contact details of someone who could help her with the funding. Mark knew people who could help with the publicity. After all, Valerie was a known name.

Soon the town was abuzz with the news and local headlines; *Valerie the Victor* was back. The support was overwhelming, and all her friends surprised her with a mini ceremony marking her return.

Valerie went on to coach athletes that would be winners at different levels. She made her come back, turned her life around, and found meaning in what she loved once again. This was possible because someone who cared for her had her back and because she accepted help. In doing so, she created a strong support system for herself that not only consisted of her friends and family but also strangers via support groups. Sometimes people you don't know can surprise you and inspire you in ways you cannot think were possible.

Strong Support System: The Catalyst for Self-worth

From Valerie's story, we can draw two important conclusions. One, while you may not always have a say in what life does to you, you have the power to accept, regroup and get back. Two, having a support system and relying on it is life-changing because they can see the beauty in us at times when we don't.

Wounded self-worth can come from anywhere, ranging from the parenting pattern in our childhood to self-imposed standards of perfection to external judgments. We know that people struggling with different degrees of self-esteem issues can struggle with mental or physical self-image issues, body image issues, perfection, or imposter syndrome, and they can find it difficult to stay resilient in the face of failures.

Mostly the story behind low self-worth can be boiled down to a feeling of being unworthy, and as a result no one will accept us or love us. This view of self-worth is directly related to the sense of having meaning in our social relationships. And while it is true our self-worth is an internal concept, not *dependent* on other people entirely, the fact of loneliness or not being accepted can surely be harmful to it. Nurturing a support system can be a strong reminder to show us that our fear of not being accepted because we are not good enough is just a fear inside our head, stopping us from fully living. During moments of extreme self-doubt and self-hate, the fierce but kind support from our loved ones might just be the thing that pulls us out of the dark pit. Insert your favorite inspirational quote on unity and togetherness here! There is a reason they exist and stir our souls.

Need more convincing? Let's look at some insights into the importance of a strong support system backed by research in different areas of mental health.

The American Psychological Association notes the importance of a strong social support system in helping people become self-reliant in coping and dealing with problems. How? By positively affecting self-worth. A supportive circle of friends and family shows trust in your abilities, which helps in focusing on problem-solving (American Psychological Association, 2022).

A study conducted by Sharaf et al. found that family and peer support plays a protective role in the lives of at-risk adolescents dealing with suicidal ideation. Not only is self-esteem higher in adolescents with high family support (including peer support as a covariate in the study), but the feeling of being cared for becomes an important factor in managing suicide-related risk behavior (Sharaf et al., 2009).

Another study by Richter et al. conducted on adolescent substance use demonstrated the qualitative impact of social support and self-esteem on the success of substance abuse treatments. Persons with a better support system have a higher chance of maintaining abstinence because they get the requisite emotional support for refusing drugs (Richter et al., 1991).

Dumont and Provost have also cited various studies that take social support as a vital element in coping with stress, mainly identifying two models to explain its role. These are the principal effect model giving people a positive context under stress, and the stress-buffering effect model, according to which a support system tempers the effect of stress (Dumont & Provost, 1999).

Through directly or indirectly having an impact on people's feeling of belongingness, support systems create the perfect environment to reclaim lost self-worth or heal a wounded one. The idea behind demonstrating its strength is to help you understand that being integrated into society serves an important emotional need of human connection. And asking for it does not make you deficient in any way. If anything, it only brings you closer to an authentic experience of being a socially embedded human being. *The self cannot be saved in isolation*!

Do you have a support system that will have your back and show you kindness when you are in need? Do you want to strengthen the ties that hold your system together? Yes, let's go!

How to Strengthen Your Support System

There are no hard and fast rules about what to do and what not to do here. The main thing to realize is that finding your people and your tribe gives you a sense of comfort and safety. People come with different communication styles, personalities, and tendencies. And all those things play a role in deciding how strong we will feel as a group.

For example, if you're going through a frustrating time in your life and you have tried the most obvious solutions present out there, someone telling you at that moment that things will eventually be alright may come across as trivializing your struggles. You may need someone to listen to you while you experience the therapeutic effect of venting without offering advice. Sometimes words of assurance can feel empty, especially while going through a sustained period of low mood. On some other occasions, you may need exactly that. Someone to remind you to have faith in things being okay eventually.

The point is, having an effective support system means relying on multiple points of support. It is also about realizing that you cannot fall back on only one person to always be available because they may have their own set of struggles. Hence, the balance lies in relying on and creating healthy boundaries with a set of people that together form a system you can count on.

Let's talk about the steps you can take to build and ensure your support system is always working for you.

Instill the Sense of Connectedness

While we are surely connected with our immediate loved ones, sometimes this may not be the case for all and/or in every situation. Additionally, stress and depression can cause us to withdraw from the world. Instilling a sense of connectedness can help us in opening up to help from our social circle. We all depend on mutual cooperation and more so in tough times. So, reach out, reach out, reach out!

Shift Your Perception of Self

The word dependence can signify some discomfort for people, especially those struggling with self-doubt and self-image issues like imposter syndrome. But it is important to realize that all words and concepts function in a specific context. Dependence doesn't have to mean loss of control or autonomy. Rather, it can mean cooperation. So, don't deny yourself the opportunity to ask for help just because your perception of self is based on the idea of unfailing strength. The hustle culture sets an unrealistic standard of being steel-minded to succeed in life. But have we ever stopped to ask why? Why should we have to be so bitterly self-sufficient that even in need and pain, we fail to ask for help? Maybe, it is time we should. It is time to create a world that understands and encourages friendships and shows up for each other in wholesome ways.

Besides, asking for help can foster a sense of community between you and your support system that is mutually beneficial and fulfilling. We will talk about every other kind of support, even customer support, but what about support for ourselves? If humans have created civilizations out of the need to socialize, a bit of reaching out will not harm you!

Reciprocity, Consideration, and Appreciation

Human relations having reciprocity and consideration at their heart, grow richer with time. The best way to have a support system is to be a support system to others too in their difficult times (Naik, 2022). Just like you can find it hard to bounce back from negative thought patterns, others can struggle with their patterns. Showing that you care goes a long way in building trust. And this trust can, in turn, make them care for you as well.

Remember the concept of mirror neurons we talked about in the first chapter? They are responsible for invoking a sense of connection and empathy. The more genuine involvement you show, making people feel they matter, the more they will feel it for you.

Similarly, acknowledging someone's support is important. It takes time and energy, and people who invest that in your well-being deserve your appreciation. It goes both ways. Even though we have an expectation from them to support us in need, it is not okay to take anyone for granted or let anyone take you for granted. Self-esteem is related to acknowledgment from our peers for our efforts. If they help you in yours, then you need to help them in theirs!

Diversify Your Circle

This is perhaps the most fun part of building a support system. Sometimes it is easier to talk to a stranger than a friend or a different friend than your normal go-to. At times, it could be a matter of not wanting to share something with someone with whom we have a history because we may not feel ready, or too overwhelmed, or simply ashamed to talk about something repeatedly.

For example, you may be thinking about venturing into online dating platforms but holding back because of some unpleasant experiences in the past. You share this with your friends, who encourage you not to let limited experiences color your entire perspective. Every time you meet, this eventually becomes a hot topic, and you feel as if you're overburdening them all the time. But you feel strongly concerned and still want to talk about it. And they have heard it so often that their response to your worries is almost automatic, making you feel partly guilty and partly annoyed at the seeming trivialization! What do you do?

You make new friends! I'm kidding. Or am I?

The idea is that sometimes having connections with people from diverse walks of life can offer you refreshingly different perspectives about your concerns and how to handle them like a pro! A fresh set of eyes can reveal a new brushstroke or a new piece of the puzzle.

So, go on, diversify, enroll in that club or that class, or start a group, find an activity, and meet people.

Bring a Professional Onboard

Perhaps the most instrumental thing you can do for yourself is to seek out professional help. Mental health practitioners and therapists don't have to be approached only when something is going wrong. They can be a valuable resource in your arsenal as trained experts in human psychology identify nuances that others may not be tuned to or in specific situations when you can't rely on someone you know (American Psychology Association, 2022).

Take the same example mentioned above. Your fear of dating can stem from a fear of investing too much and being emotionally hurt, or you can struggle with maintaining healthy boundaries. A trained professional can help chart out a path backed by scientific research offering a comprehensive solution to your specific needs.

Sometimes when no one can indeed be reached, your dedicated therapist can be. It is an excellent safety net to fall back on for constructive and conscious self-development.

Let the Toxic Ones Go

When it comes to establishing a strong support system, flagging the toxicity that can sometimes accompany relations is imperative. It would be a mistake to talk about support without taking into account the emotional harm toxic people can do to us. Chapter 2 touched upon the theme of developing healthy patterns in relationships. When possible, let them go; when not, minimize your involvement. Toxicity doesn't happen suddenly and may reveal itself over many painful years sometimes, but regardless of the time taken, letting go is an act of unburdening yourself that is worth it. It is all the more relevant when toxic people expect you to come through for them without respecting your space and energy.

How can you achieve this in practice? Two key ingredients:

- Setting healthy boundaries.

- Normalizing saying no.

Since support systems are mutual in nature, people will count on you to be there for them too. This can especially be a muddled-up situation when the people in question don't understand your boundaries.

Let's say you don't appreciate humor that is based on depreciating someone's mental health problems, and your friend has a tendency to make a joke every time you are together. You feel really strongly about it. After telling them politely a bunch of times, it seems pointless to bring it up again only to be disregarded. It triggers you and does not align with the values you hold dear. They, on the other hand, go on to belittle you for taking everything to heart.

A friend truly respecting your sensibilities will be mindful of respecting your choices and reduce such jokes, if not completely eliminating them in your presence. If they are not doing so, rather gaslighting you by asking you to just relax, they are revealing just how little they think of matters important to you.

In such cases where you don't feel seen or heard, it is best to let such people go. Surrounding yourself with people that drain you or don't respect your boundaries can have a negative impact on your self-worth.

Similarly, knowing when to say no and excusing yourself from people who would unload their problems and struggles on you without any consideration for your mental space can leave you feeling exhausted. Yes, you should try to help the people you love, but that does not mean being available by compromising on your needs or peace of mind. Besides, you cannot help anyone without first making sure you're alright.

Alternatively, saying no does not mean running away from your responsibilities or commitments but is an act of self-care. Sometimes you may not be in a situation to help someone or give them your time immediately for a number of reasons. People who respect you will always allow your space. And you can come back to them when you are ready. Saying no will only mean that when you do show up, you are actually available and help in a better way.

Letting go of people and things is not easy, especially if they have been a constant part of your life. And when you are someone facing problems with self-worth and prone to pleasing people, it is doubly hard. The ultimate way to ensure you are nurturing a supportive ecosystem for yourself is to know who you are and what you need. This is where self-awareness assumes a pivotal role. In a way, self-awareness has been a recurring theme throughout this book, and it's time to turn our focus more directly toward it with the next chapter.

With that, we come to the end of this chapter. Can you think of ways to strengthen the support system in your life? Perhaps, write an appreciation letter to someone who has been your rock!

Chapter 7:

Three Gifts of Self-Awareness: Gratitude, Forgiveness, and Letting Go

The curious paradox is that when I accept myself just as I am, then I change. –Carl R Rogers

Remember the question we began the introduction with? Let's modify that a little and ask another one. Do you know who you are? Are you aware of yourself? If I were to give you a piece of paper and ask you to give me the most comprehensive introduction, what would you write about? Will you tell me your hopes and fears, or maybe your achievements? Will you tell me about the core memories that drive you?

When we come to think of self-awareness, the knowledge of ourselves we are trying to seek goes beyond the usual introduction. Self-awareness is the process of knowing the deepest motivations and triggering factors behind our behavior, hopes, and fears.

It is being aware of the emotions and sensations that accompany our lived experiences. It is a self-reflexive activity involving pondering the question of who you are as a human being and the values that define you. It is also a way to connect with your body and mind consciously.

You may stop and ask, I know myself, don't I? I live in my body and use my brain; how come they are anything but connected?

Psychology and neuroscience research can provide some valuable insights in this area. Dr. Nicole LePera explains that, quite often than not, our thoughts and behavior are motivated by patterns imprinted in our minds long ago, sometimes going back to childhood. These patterns may lead us to bury a part of ourselves somewhere away from the light of conscious awareness, affecting our actions and coping mechanisms, all to keep us feeling safe without our conscious knowledge (LePera, 2022). Additionally, the experience of a traumatic event can keep us physically and mentally locked in a state of extreme stress as our body and mind perceive the danger that may not be actually present, making us relive the event and act accordingly (van der Kolk, 2014). This is often the result of our brains acting like scanners for threats and amplifying anticipations to prepare us for survival.

The lesson for us is to learn that certain parts of our psyche can significantly impact the quality of our life and the reality we experience. When it comes to self-doubt and self-worth, these parts can keep us stuck in a cycle of negative ruminations. It can lead to emotional dysregulation, insecurities, and dissociation (LePera, 2022). Recall Jonathan and his negative spiral. A life that is meant to be enjoyed authentically becomes a nightmare to be survived. Unless we illuminate that which stays hidden, we cannot hope to bring a positive change in our lives.

Self-awareness brings light to those shadow aspects of us, as Dr. LePera calls them, which are out of the mind's sight, but very much present and active, waiting to be acknowledged. And by doing so, we can integrate them fully into our reality, accepting and loving them as, ultimately, they make up the whole of us (LePera, 2022). This can help in navigating the *possibility* and the *paradox* of change! Why the paradox? Because even though neuroscience shows evidence of neuroplasticity (the ability to rewire the brain by forming new neural pathways), the brain's threat-detecting part, the amygdala, loves certainty, control, and predictability in order to feel safe, making new change uncomfortable (van der Kolk, 2014; LePera, 2022).

So, how can we become self-aware in a fruitful manner to initiate a personal transformation? There are a number of paths to strengthen the connection between body and mind with the intention of fostering self-observation of thought patterns.

Paths to Self-Awareness

If you google self-awareness techniques, you can find a plethora of information, including creative techniques to help you guide along the way. Many of these practices are overlapping and common knowledge. But the primary thing to focus on is mindfulness and being grounded while you follow those techniques. Along with that, it is equally important to be patient. Acknowledging and facing ourselves can be an overwhelming process and lead to cathartic emotional release. Remember to show yourself compassion and let everything flow as it happens. This is the only way to let things happen organically and authentically. Let's do it!

Doing Nothing but Doing Everything: The Wisdom in Stillness

Let me share a powerful quote from the movie *Kung Fu Panda* that you may have heard before. It goes, "Your mind is like this water, my friend. When it is agitated, it becomes difficult to see. But if you allow it to settle, the answer becomes clear." (Stevenson & Osborne, 2008, 0:07:28).

They say animation is for kids, but I promise you there is nothing kiddish about this quote or the movie! Coming from Master Oogway, the wise old teacher seemingly having access to the mysteries of the universe, this quote encapsulates the core of self-awareness. It can serve as a beacon of insight, revealing a simple truth that all the answers you're looking for are hidden within you.

When you're being pulled in different directions of self-doubt, uncertainty, fear, and anxiety, your strengths and skills can be obscured. Cultivating some stillness and silence can help you uncover yourself more objectively.

Why is this important? As we grow up, we learn things that become muscle memory. That means we go through the motions without giving much thought to the actual actions. For example, you wake up and brush your teeth. You don't think about the muscles involved or the motion of your hand, or the process of squeezing out the paste onto your brush. They just become habits. Similarly, our thoughts can function on autopilot, too (LePera, 2022).

These patterns are a shortcut built to access relevant information quickly. The process is hidden to reduce the stress of going back to basics repeatedly. But this shortcut is a double-edged sword. There is no way for the brain mechanism itself to know which of our habits and thought cycles are beneficial or bad for us. That is the function of our conscious rational faculty.

This autopilot mode keeps us stuck in our repetitive cycles, making decisions that are safe and predictable. So, the function of this first exercise in stillness is to catch hold of this autopilot mode and bring conscious awareness to it by becoming present in the moment.

Stillness can be uncomfortable at first and feel like a confrontation with your negative thoughts that have more power than you. So, it is imperative to remember not to rush into it. Take baby steps to get into the habit of connecting with yourself. You can start with just five minutes. The focus here is to bring your awareness to now by following these simple steps:

- Take a pause and relax (we will discuss some relaxation and breathing techniques in the next section, but you can choose any technique that relaxes you).

- Find a quiet place in your home, a room, or a corner, or if you prefer the outdoors, somewhere you will not be disturbed directly.

- Slowly bring your attention to your five senses of sight, smell, hearing, touch, and taste in any order you prefer.

- Spend a few moments feeling what your senses are feeling.

- Once you have established a connection and safety within your body, move to your thoughts, traveling inwards.

- Bring your attention to the loudest, most significant thought you have at that moment.

- Just observe it but don't attach any good or bad value to it. Let it flow the way it flows.

- Hold it for a few seconds and then release it, bringing your attention back to your five senses and returning to the world.

Once you are done, you can make a note of that thought. It can help you see more clearly whatever it is that is having the strongest influence on you. If it's a positive thought, nurture it; if it's a negative one, use the techniques mentioned in the fourth chapter to challenge negative self-talk and thought patterns.

Apart from giving you a tool for self-awareness, this practice can help you release stress and feel centered by releasing thoughts trapped under the surface of consciousness.

Breathe In, Breathe Out

What is more basic than breathing? And yet, there is more to it than just inhaling and exhaling. When we are stressed or anxious, our bodies tense up, causing restricted flow of oxygen to our lungs, causing a further spike in the heart rate. Conscious breathwork can help with that by lowering the heart rate and effectively managing stress (Harvard Health Publishing, 2020). Think of it as breathing in reassurance and exhaling fear.

Conscious deep breathing creates a state of calm which is important when connecting with the inner self. There are a number of ways to practice conscious breathing, offering different patterns and rhythms of inhalation and exhalation. You can choose whichever you feel comfortable to start with. The essence of all those different techniques is:

- focused, deep, and slow breaths filling up your lungs and belly

- unrestricted and organic flow of breath by relaxing tensed muscles of the body

You can also browse through guided online meditation videos or yoga practices focusing primarily on breathwork. Dr. LePera lists some breathing practices in great detail, like balanced breathing, where you inhale and exhale for five seconds; deep belly breathing, where you place your hands on your belly to feel its rise and fall with your breathing; and 4-7-8 breathing, where you inhale for four seconds, hold it for seven seconds, and exhale for eight seconds (LePera, 2022).

This last technique can take some getting used to, but there is no hard and fast rule around the number of seconds you need to inhale or exhale for as long as you do so deeply. You are absolutely free and encouraged to come up with your own practice!

Another widely popular and documented technique that can be used with conscious breathing is progressive muscle relaxation. Nick Trenton (2021, p. 60) has explained this technique as "taking control of your muscles, to deliberately loosen and relax them."

It's a simple process he explains:

- Get comfortable in a position of your choosing, sitting or standing with eyes closed (or open, depending on your comfort).

- Starting from the top or bottom, bring your attention to different body parts one after the other, like your feet, calves, thighs, and so on.

- Tighten the muscles as much as you can while being mindful of not causing injury or cramps.

- Hold for a few seconds as per your comfort.

- Let go and relax the muscles completely in a sudden fashion. Move on to the next focus area and continue until the whole body is relaxed.

To make it more engaging and stimulating, Trenton suggests visualization of the process (Trenton, 2021). You can create any imagery. For example, you can imagine yourself melting away like chocolate ice cream, softening up like velvet, or even becoming light like fluffy clouds!

Asking Questions and Observing Time

This is where we focus on asking ourselves certain questions aimed at better understanding ourselves. This is also where we observe our time usage throughout the day. I want to remind you here that you must do this from a place of being neutral and gentle.

There are two parts to this activity. The first one is a bit like journaling but comparatively more pointed, as here you will ask specific questions. You can do this any time of the day. You can grab a notebook for it or use your computer, laptop, or mobile, whichever is comfortable. It is okay if you don't know the answers completely and immediately; you can take your time. There are no perfect absolute answers, and they evolve as you progress on your self-awareness journey. Here are the questions:

- Do I have a fair idea of my priorities and needs?

- Do I know how I want people to show up for me when I need help?

- Do I have a clear sense of what brings me peace and contentment?

- Do I know what activities bring me joy and help me rejuvenate?

- Does my life as it is now align with my values?

- Do I take the time to learn new things and evolve?

- How often do I become overburdened and stressed, and what do I do about it?

- What do I feel when I am unsuccessful at something? How does my body react to it?

- How do I react when I am sad, happy, or angry?

- How frequently do I feel my reactions to adverse situations could have been better?

- Am I able to stand my ground and do what I believe in, or do I go by the ideas of someone else?

These questions can reveal so much to you, both in terms of what you know and don't know. We will see the counterpart of this exercise a little later.

The second part of this activity is to be mindful of how you spend most of your time. Your routine can reveal to you whether you are living consciously, facing and dealing with stressors, or avoiding them. For example, if you procrastinate on some work that is potentially stressful in order to binge-watch your favorite series, you may create more anxiety around the completion of that task.

Here too, you can keep a time journal, tracking your daily activities and when you engage in them. An important part of this is also taking note of what you were doing, reading, and watching just before you started feeling anxious or weighed down.

Ground Your Body, Move Your Body

No, I promise this is not about some grueling physical exercise! The movement here has an entirely different purpose. We are sustained by a constant flow of energy within our bodies. The idea of moving around is to prevent our energy from becoming stagnant and do it with conscious attention to the body.

If you are familiar with the polyvagal theory, great. But if not, let me briefly tell you about it. The polyvagal theory explains the role of the vagus nerve in calming us as part of our autonomic nervous system (the one that controls involuntary functions like heartbeat, breathing, blinking, and so on). There are two parts of our autonomous nervous system: sympathetic and parasympathetic. The former controls fight-or-flight responses, and the latter controls rest and digest phases. The vagus nerve, which is part of the parasympathetic nervous system, plays a role in getting our body back to baseline normal functioning when we feel safe. But when our bodies store trauma, we can be stuck in a cycle of fight-or-flight response leading to constant reliving of that trauma (Porges, 2011; van der Kolk, 2014).

Therefore, it becomes important to realize that our bodies need to release the stored stress, and grounding and movement become excellent ways to achieve that.

Grounding is a way to anchor ourselves in our body and establish a secure connection with it. It can help us in coming back to ourselves in a reassuring way especially in times of anxiety or panic attacks. The 5-4-3-2-1 method (Medical News Today, 2020) is a popular grounding technique where you look for:

- five things you can see

- four things you can touch

- three things you can hear

- two things you can smell

- one thing you can taste

When it comes to movement, you can choose any form ranging from stretching, walking, dancing, or energy-focused practices like tai chi. When you engage in any movement, focus on how each part of your body feels. Pay attention to the range of motion of your arms and legs, the way your muscles move, constrict and release, and how your joints feel. If you dance, feel the rhythm and beat and focus on how your body moves in coordination.

Body movement is also meaningful from the point of view of self-esteem and body image issues. Often people struggling with confidence in their bodies can restrict themselves, hiding what they think are their flaws. It can manifest in faulty posture, conscious gait, and wardrobe choices that *hide* unwanted parts of our bodies.

But allowing yourself to move can help you take up the space that your beautiful body deserves. Try engaging with your body in front of the mirror, whether through exercise or dance, and really look at yourself while letting yourself free. See the incredible ability of your body to carry you through life.

Remembering You Are Nature

Connecting with nature can be a profound experience. Studies have shown being in nature has a positive effect on relieving stress, and releasing happy hormones like serotonin and dopamine (LePera, 2022). There is a reason why cultures of the world impart the wisdom of spending time in the sun, feeling the earth, being near the water, or in a forest. The sun isn't just to obtain vitamin D, nor is the forest only for fresh oxygen! So, take out some time to allow your skin to feel the warmth of our big yellow friend in the sky or the coolness and freshness of the wind and water.

You can choose to connect with nature in a way that appeals to you most. It can usher in a meditative state without you needing to sit down formally to meditate. And the same principles of being in the present moment apply here. Allow nature to create a whole sensory and ambient experience for you.

Connecting with nature can also nurture a sense of belongingness. At least, this is what Josh and Anna realized. They were both avid campers. As they went trekking through the Himalayas, they came across a beautiful mountain lake surrounded by lush greenery. Tired and sweaty from their hike, they decided to wash their faces with the cool water and rest for some time before continuing.

As they were relaxing, Anna got lost in thought, watching the birds flying over to the other side of the lake. She told Josh how marvelous she thought this whole moment was. The water that was sustenance to humans was sustenance to all life forms. In that moment, they both realized they were part of something much larger. They were not only connected to nature; they *were* nature.

If you go back to your science class and remember that lecture on evolution, you can arrive at the same conclusion. It's just a matter of perspective! Shift the narrative, and you will see you are not alone. You are already connected to people and everything else that our earth has to offer. In tough times, this can help in finding a sense of reassurance.

You belong! And you're every bit as worthy as this precious ecosystem you're a part of.

Self-Awareness Comes Bearing Gifts

When you move along the path of self-awareness, you will not only reaffirm your humanity but also the things you are blessed with. Yes, it will take time and will not be an easy journey, but it will be worth it.

Gratitude

The purpose of self-awareness is to embrace yourself entirely. This acceptance brings gratitude toward the world and yourself. When you realize that life is a mixed bag of challenges and opportunities, you are faced with a choice. You may not always be in control of external environments, but you can decide how your internal environment will be and its responses to the outside. By living on autopilot, your subconscious mind will make that choice for you. But once you start living consciously, you will make that choice for yourself.

As you move forward with challenges with a shift in perspective, you allow yourself to see how they cause discomfort but also lead to *growth*. And that, my friend, is a road to gratitude.

Understood as a feeling of thankfulness toward the benefits, gifts, or good things within us and outside that enable us to form a connection and make life worth living, gratitude brings greater emotional and social well-being (Millacci, 2017). Because you are interconnected with everything else around you, there is a relationship of interdependence. This interdependence is what allows us to talk about community and strengthens support systems.

Just like self-awareness, gratitude is also a choice. You can *choose* to look for things that make you happy even when it's hard to do so. *It serves an important function of keeping hope alive.* And only a self-aware, perceptive mind that looks beyond the surface will recognize the myriad little things to be thankful for, like the ground beneath your feet, the friend who shows up for you, and the heart that beats everyday!

Here is how you can nourish and express gratitude in your life:

- Take the time to mindfully acknowledge all things, big or small, that bring you joy.

- Understand that joy can be as simple as completing daily tasks or feeling the cool breeze on your face after a hot day.

- Acknowledge the help and thoughtfulness of your loved ones and friends.

- Include a daily gratitude practice in your life through a gratitude journal or a few mindful moments to sit in that feeling and let it wash over you.

- Whatever happened to good old handwritten letters? They're a lovely way to connect with yourself and others. Expressing thankfulness by writing letters yourself can transfer that feeling of joy from you to the recipient, continuing the gratitude cycle.

- Shift your perspective from lack to abundance. Focus on what you have and how you can grow it.

Forgiveness

With self-awareness and gratitude comes forgiveness. Most importantly, the act of forgiving yourself. In our journey to this point, hopefully you can identify how people can carry the burden of blame, guilt, shame, and anger for things that are never their fault, to begin with.

Whether it is the pressure of perfectionism that comes with imposter syndrome or the fear of failure, attaching your worth completely to your achievements or other people's opinion of you erects unrealistic expectations. When you fail to meet such expectations, the whole network of feelings we talked about in the first two chapters gets activated, and your distorted thoughts can run the show.

However, our journey has been one of unlearning. Reclaiming self-worth is as much about learning to love yourself as it is about unlearning the patterns of negative thoughts about yourself. When all is said and done, you have to forgive yourself with kindness and compassion. Forgive because you are learning and growing, and mistakes are a natural part of the human experience. You can put down the weight you are carrying and let it go.

Speaking of burdens, forgiveness in an interpersonal environment is also equally as essential. There can be times when someone's actions can be unjust toward us and hurt us. Allow yourself to feel that hurt and grief and process it. But once processed, forgive them and those circumstances as well. Sometimes, even our primary caregivers need to be forgiven. They may not always know the best. Forgiving them can bring a sense of closure.

It is important to know that forgiveness is never about the other person. It is about our own selves. Holding on to the hurts of the past can take up so much energy and space in your mental universe that you can be consumed by it. It only holds you back from bouncing back to your original, happy self. Forgiveness offers a path to release everything that no longer aligns with your highest good to make space for new experiences.

So, using one of the techniques mentioned in the previous sections, ask yourself what you need to forgive and make peace with. You can use these prompts to get started, but remember, it is all open to you the way you want to approach it:

- How do I feel about that negative experience in the past (you can choose the incident you want to heal)?

- Am I holding on to any grudges from the past?

- Does something that happened in the past still affect my actions beyond a point?

- Am I preoccupied with the hurt of the past?

- Do the memories of that event still invoke feelings as if I am going through it all over again?

- Can I do something to transform these feelings?

This last question brings us to the next related gift of self-awareness. The act of letting go.

Letting Go

Self-awareness teaches us the balance between control and letting go. Have you ever wondered about the objects you hold onto in life? Maybe belongings for the purpose of nostalgia, or things of monetary value, or even relationships that no longer fulfill you? You are not alone in doing that.

Things and people, in a way, become inextricably linked to our self-identity and what we stand for. They act like a security blanket to cover us when the cold of the uncertainty of this vast world hits us. They are like our anchors, keeping us in familiar territory.

But we don't only hold on to external things and people. We also hold on to our thoughts and feelings, especially the negative ones, because they are what we have known for the longest time, and they offer us the security of certainty. If I already anticipate a negative outcome, I will never take the risk. But what we forget is that no matter how much we try to do things exactly by the book or perfectly, some things are uncontrollable. There is no way of ensuring any kind of guarantee of happiness and sadness. And the more we try to control outcomes, the more upset we feel when things don't go our way. This is not an effective way to live a fulfilling life. Being in control takes away the beauty of surprises and the joy of existing when all you do is worry about the things beyond us.

Of course, it doesn't mean you should not try anything if nothing is in your control. That is the other extreme of this conundrum. The point is to find a golden middle path, like Aristotle's golden mean between two extremes, an intermediate path (Kraut, 2022).

Letting go is supposed to be challenging. It takes tremendous strength to make peace with the giving up of control. If we remember that the tradeoff is worth it, deep peace in this case, we can slowly cultivate a sense of calm and acceptance in our lives. In a way, forgiveness and letting go are connected. As we let go of expectations and make peace with our past, we can bring forth a childlike energy in our endeavors that is curious and playful.

So, tell yourself it's okay. You'll be okay. I'll be okay.

Chapter 8:

Maintaining Strong Self-Worth: Welcoming Your Authentic Self

We have now come to the end of our journey! Are you ready to welcome your authentic self into the light? I am excited as you are! You now have all the tools you will need to embrace yourself with love and create a transformed version of yourself. When you consciously take your place at the center stage of your life and express yourself with integrity regardless of the judgments and opinions of others, you reflect on your authentic self.

However, change comes with challenges. There is one last set of tools I want to empower you with so you can deal with these challenges effectively without feeling like you have to give up. Using these tools, you can maintain a positive and healthy relationship with yourself.

But first, let's identify the challenges that you can potentially face:

- resistance to unfamiliar ways of being

- avoiding the discomfort of self-work in favor of a comfortable self-identity, even if it restricts you

- doubting the effectiveness of self-love

- expecting permanent and absolute guarantees and losing hope

- thinking of mindful living as a temporary fix

- seeking external validation for your healing journey and second-guessing yourself

- gaslighting yourself into thinking you seek attention and don't deserve self-love

- difficulty in forgiving, reconciling, and letting go of strong negative emotions

- struggle with the guilt of maintaining your boundaries and prioritizing your needs

- struggle with the choice of letting things and people go that don't align with your authentic self

Remember that our brains are lovers of predictable patterns to ensure safety. These challenges will plunge you into the deep end of the self-work swimming pool, but with consistent effort, you will learn to swim. Is it true? Are you thinking, what if you drown before learning? That won't happen because I promise you, the pool is only a mirage. The closer you get to your goals, the more you will see clearly. You have got this. You have everything you need to become your best friend and foremost cheerleader.

Take this quick guide as a checklist for when you are feeling overwhelmed and close to giving up. Look at it and look at all the mind-blowing work you have done till now and the narrative you have shifted. Believe in yourself because only you can, and that matters the most.

Self-Compassion

When you first start on your journey, your negative thought patterns and neural pathways connected to them will be the strongest. It will be so natural then to feel the force of the world against you. This is where you will need an unconditional amount of self-love and self-compassion.

Conjure up the image of a toddler learning to walk. Imagine all the times they may have fallen, stumbled, and gotten back up. If that little toddler could do it, you, a grown-up, can too. Remember, it is only as we grow up that we recognize limitations and failures. You can employ any imagination that inspires you. You can also devise strategies to show yourself compassion.

Dr. LePera suggests various strategies like telling yourself words of encouragement, reassuring yourself, and even utilizing the power of self-soothing touch. Self-soothing behavior involves keeping your hands gently over your chest and breathing deeply, connecting with the rise and fall of your body. Imagine yourself soothing your heart and relaxing into the rhythm (LePera, 2022). You can also hug yourself to recreate the feeling of being held. There is something very powerful about your own capacity to heal yourself.

Additionally, you can use affirmations of self-love in the morning or before bed or write yourself letters at different points in time, to be found later.

Take the Win

Continuing with the same theme, initial difficulties can make you question the efficacy of your efforts. Remember, the expectation of perfection and success in the first go was the cause for self-doubt in the first place. Conscious living is not a miracle or a matter of luck. It takes developing a habit, much like everything else.

So, it becomes crucial to show yourself the appreciation you deserve for showing up consistently. Take the wins, and celebrate them, even if they seem small. Show yourself the reward for trying and make the neural pathways connected to this new habit stronger by practice.

There are a couple of ways you can show yourself some genuine appreciation:

- Take yourself out for a nice lunch/dinner.

- Show yourself your favorite movie.

- Buy yourself some nice flowers.

- Share your daily wins with your loved ones.

- Hug yourself for your fantastic efforts.

Remind yourself that slipping back is not failure. Nothing is a failure. It is only learning and growing. It is not supposed to be a linear journey, and abandoning shame and guilt to honor yourself will help you stay motivated.

Underscore the Role of Rest

Perennial self-doubters know well that resting under a deadline can feel like cheating on your work. Remember the two poles of imposter syndrome we discussed in the third chapter? This one is for all those folks out there who put themselves under an enormous amount of stress to achieve perfection. The self-imposed standard of productivity will be hard to let go of as you begin taking conscious breaks from an environment valuing hustle culture.

You will feel a pull toward going back to your old ways of being. But remember, rest is not cheating. It is a fundamental condition of existence. Looking at it from a cyclical perspective offers a more holistic way to integrate rest into your life and gives you a sense of connectedness with everything else around you. Think about how you are connected to the earth. How one part of it sees the light of the day as the other relaxes in the night.

Even if you are someone that follows the night owl life and doesn't relate to the day and night analogy, understand that your body will need rest. The good part about mindful living is getting the chance to make that decision for yourself. So, choose to incorporate periods of rest in your life to avoid burnout. It is okay to take the time to rejuvenate and regroup and come back with renewed vigor. If anything, disengaging allows you to see the big picture at times and may offer you lightbulb moments to perform better at work or at anything holding your attention at the moment.

It is also necessary to remember that being mindful can take a toll if you allow yourself to be stressed about it! The whole reason you began this journey was to live more meaningfully by reducing stress. If you have a tendency to overwork, you may likely feel the need to overwork conscious living too! It will have a totally counterintuitive effect.

So, accept that some days will still be hard, and you may not get a chance to follow through with your routine of self-care perfectly. It's okay because mindfulness is about allowing you the space to tweak what works for you. Rest, and then get back.

Let Go of Self-Censorship, Embrace YOLO

Low self-esteem can cause us to hide our true selves and curtail our self-expression for a number of reasons. If you grew up in an environment of parental neglect or dealt with a negative body image, retreating back into yourself may have felt like the only safe option. Constant comparisons may have solidified this behavior.

For your authentic self to break free, you will have to confront the myths of self-worth. You can show yourself that it is safe to come out now. You have nothing to apologize for. What's more, expressing your truth is a way to explore your personality. Many of us deny ourselves the chance to experiment and know who we truly are in order to fit in or seek the approval of our peers or family.

Authenticity will require you to explore what it means to you. You can use the questions aimed at building self-awareness to find out who you are as a person. But remember, you are not a marble statue, static. Your self is not fixed, and it will keep evolving with time. So, keep up the self-reflexive work going, and hold your autonomy dear.

Authenticity will also lead you to challenge your tendency to please people. Don't be afraid of this challenge. Meet it head-on, and I promise that you will pull through with a greater sense of satisfaction. When we stop alienating ourselves, we unlock a new dimension of living. After all, you only live once, so embrace the YOLO.

If you live in a physically abusive and/or emotionally unsafe space where it's unsafe to be your true self, don't hesitate to reach out for help from your support system or professional mental health practitioners.

Go Visual

Now that we have talked about self-exploration to reveal your authentic self, the next level is to envision yourself. This is a popular technique used by the self-help community. Invoking visuals and feelings of your future authentic self can be a powerful transformative tool (LePera, 2022).

Think of directing the movie of your life. Visualize every aspect of your being. What do you do for a living? Where do you stay? What do you feel? Do this as if you are already experiencing this reality. Engaging with this visual can send strong messages to your subconscious mind.

Try this:

- Find a quiet place and practice some deep breathing to connect with your inner self.

- Now imagine a scene from your distant future. It could be anything, day or night, home or place of work.

- Notice the way you move through. Feel the emotions that invoke a sense of satisfaction and happiness.

- Imagine what it feels like to have your version of a successful life.

- Imagine a conversation between you and another person. A friend, family member, or a colleague.

- How are they treating you? What is the manner in which they are speaking to you?

- Imagine how you are taking care of yourself, performing day-to-day activities like cooking for yourself, keeping your space tidy, and folding your clothes.

- Imagine all this as powerfully as possible and slowly extract it to bring it back with you to the present moment.

When we bring the reality of how we want to be closer to us, our brains can show us the way to make it achievable. Think about how the negative self-perpetuating cycle of self-doubt caused Jonathan from the first chapter to act in exactly the way he wanted to avoid. If unhealthy thoughts can predispose us to behave in ways that fulfill a self-imposed prophecy of doom, healthy thoughts can encourage us to do the opposite.

Of course, it is not some magical spell that will conjure up reality from thoughts. But it sure is an effective tool to set intentions and goals, which are the beginning of any transformation. Maybe, magical indeed from a different perspective!

Feel All the Feelings

Mindfulness talk can sound like toxic positivity. But reclaiming your self-worth does not mean pushing your supposed negative aspects away and suppressing them. That would be a lie you tell yourself. Let yourself be open to every feeling without being attached to anyone in particular. Give a nod to all of it, and then keep moving ahead. Honor every phase you are in and know that it will not last.

Shutting them out only buries them under a rug. Integrating them into the field of your self-awareness and acceptance minimizes your chances of a complete breakdown. Because you know yourself and accept vulnerability as natural and human, you embody the word authentic *authentically*!

Embracing your imperfections and strengths is a show of unconditional self-love. It is where your self-worth will derive its internal validation from. So, tell yourself with kindness that it's okay to feel sad on some days. It's alright to feel afraid. You are resilient enough to carry on and turn your challenges into your gifts.

Honor Your Authentic Values

Lastly, self-worth relies on your ability to set healthy boundaries that align with your values. But what are your values?

Defining what matters to you is a crucial step, perhaps the most important, to live authentically. At first, it may seem very hard. Spending a major chunk of our life absorbing perceptions of good and bad, acceptable and unacceptable, fed to us by the media, societal norms, family, and community conditions us to take them at face value. Sometimes, even when we know better, uncritically accepting them seems like the only way to be accepted as an insider in a community. Belongingness is a basic social need.

But being self-aware will inevitably lead you to ask yourself what values are dear to you. What worldview resonates with you? In a way, we all are our own personal philosophers. Try this strategy to gain an insight into what values are meaningful to you:

- Take note of how you feel you can help people in the best way and why. This can show you want qualities you value.

- Recall incidents from your life when you felt inspired by someone, and why.

- Recall incidents from your life when you felt strong disapproval for someone or something, and why.

- Imagine a world problem you would like to solve. Ask yourself what the leaders are missing so that you can show them.

- Think about the big questions of the world in terms of freedoms, rights, organization and functioning of the society, and relations between diverse communities.

- Think of how you want to be treated by the people around you. Can you imagine a universal basic set of values you would want everyone to have?

As your values become clearer, you will find another hurdle that we saw in one of the challenges discussed above. The challenge of choosing to let people that don't respect your values go. But the stronger you become in your resolve to live with your personal truth, the easier it will become to draw healthy boundaries.

Now that you are equipped with all you need to know, it's time to turn the page, shift the narrative!

Conclusion

We began this journey by taking a closer look at self-doubt and wounded self-worth and their causes. From childhood traumas and past experiences to environmental factors, we identified triggers that keep us stuck in unhealthy patterns and hold us back from living a happy and fulfilling life. We also understood and demolished the myths associated with self-worth and found them to be a product of distorted socio-cultural as well as personal projections.

Making sense of imposter syndrome reveals to us the importance of recognizing and effectively challenging negative self-talk, confronting our fear of failure, and building resilience.

While negative self-talk makes us believe we are not adequate enough and incapable of changing our circumstances, questioning this talk helps in detaching ourselves from it. We are not our problems, and our thoughts are not always an accurate reflection of reality. Dealing with negative self-talk by replacing it with a growth mindset brings us closer to accepting ourselves. By showing failures to be mistakes, a natural part of learning new things, the growth mindset shifts our focus from immediate perfection to consistent effort. Consistency and resilience are the pillars of growth.

While only we have to live through our ups and downs, the ability to empathize with others allows us to create a community of shared interests. This community supports us. Support systems are networks we can fall back on in times of need. Not only do they provide emotional belongingness, but they also lift us up, as we saw in Valerie's story. They show us our strengths when we fail to see them.

Self-awareness is a key piece of the puzzle in our quest to reclaim our self-worth and embrace ourselves unconditionally. Practicing mindfulness invokes a deep sense of calm and confidence by bringing us back to ourselves. It helps us unlearn and relearn important facets of ourselves. This serves the function of invoking feelings of gratitude.

Gratitude imbues us with hope, and forgiveness lets us release the burdens of the past, including hurt and anger that may be affecting our self-worth.

You have what it takes to follow through and start living the life you secretly dream of. You are worthy and every bit deserving of love and strength. Nothing will hold you back from fully blossoming into your true self when you decide to take conscious control of your thoughts and actions. It is not a promise that all your troubles will be gone forever, but it is a promise that as and when they arrive, you will have the grit to face them and successfully make it to the other side. Sure, life will throw up challenges, but you will be wiser in knowing that they are just here to qualify you to the next level.

Now make a promise to yourself that you will live your authentic truth. You will carry the lessons you have learned here and let go of that constantly chattering monkey-brain voice that has made you hold on to limiting beliefs. Become your ardent fan, and keep your eyes open. Become the gatekeeper of your mental health if you have to, armed with the powers of self-compassion. Make a solemn resolve to show up for yourself every day.

You can. You will.

References

Ackerman, C. (2017, March 20). *25 CBT techniques and worksheets for cognitive behavioral therapy.* PositivePsychology.com. https://positivepsychology.com/cbt-cognitive-behavioral-therapy-techniques-worksheets/

American Psychological Association. (2017, July). *What is cognitive behavioral therapy?* https://www.apa.org/ptsd-guideline/patients-and-families/cognitive-behavioral

American Psychological Association. (2022, October 21). *Manage stress: Strengthen your support network.* https://www.apa.org/topics/stress/manage-social-support

Bleidorn, W., Arslan, R. C., Denissen, J. J. A., Rentfrow, P. J., Gebauer, J. E., Potter, J., & Gosling, S. D. (2016). Age and gender differences in self-esteem—A cross-cultural window. *Journal of Personality and Social Psychology, 111*(3), 396–410. https://doi.org/10.1037/pspp0000078

Braslow, M. D., Guerrettaz, J., Arkin, R. M., & Oleson, K. C. (2012). Self-Doubt. *Social and Personality Psychology Compass, 6*(6), 470–482.

https://doi.org/10.1111/j.1751-9004.2012.00441.x

Budiarto, Y., & Helmi, A. F. (2021). Shame and self-esteem: A meta-analysis. *Europe's Journal of Psychology,* *17*(2), 131–145. https://doi.org/10.5964/ejop.2115

Consiglio, I., & van Osselaer, S. M. J. (2022). The effects of consumption on self-esteem. *Current Opinion in Psychology,* *46*, 101341. https://doi.org/10.1016/j.copsyc.2022.101341

Dumont, M., & Provost, M. A. (1999). Resilience in adolescents: Protective role of social support, coping strategies, self-esteem, and social activities on experience of stress and depression. *Journal of Youth and Adolescence, 28*(3), 343–363. https://doi.org/10.1023/a:1021637011732

Dweck, C. S. (2006). *Mindset: The new psychology of success.* Random House.

Dye, H. (2018). The impact and long-term effects of childhood trauma. *Journal of Human Behavior in the Social Environment, 28*(3), 381–392. https://doi.org/10.1080/10911359.2018.1435328

Golden, B. (2023, January 28). *How do self-esteem and related factors impact anger arousal?* Psychology Today.

https://www.psychologytoday.com/us/blog/o
vercoming-destructive-anger/202301/how-do-
self-esteem-and-related factors-impact-anger

Harvard Health Publishing. (2020, July 6). *Relaxation techniques: Breath control helps quell errant stress response.* https://www.health.harvard.edu/mind-and-mood/relaxation-techniques-breath-control-helps-quell-errant-stress-response

Hay, L. L. (1984). *You can heal your life.* Full Circle.

Hermann, A. D., Leonardelli, G. J., & Arkin, R. M. (2002). Self-Doubt and self-esteem: A threat from within. *Personality and Social Psychology Bulletin,* *28*(3), 395–408. https://doi.org/10.1177/0146167202286010

Hibberd, J. (2019). *The imposter cure: How to stop feeling like a fraud and escape the mind-trap of imposter syndrome.* Aster.

Hodari, A. J., Tutu, A. D., & Sobers, Y. M. (2013). *Lifelines : the black book of proverbs.* Broadway Books.

Kraut, R. (2018). *Aristotle's Ethics.* Stanford Encyclopedia of Philosophy. https://plato.stanford.edu/entries/aristotle-ethics/

Lachmann, S. (2013, December 24). *10 sources of low self-esteem: What happened as you grew up was not your fault.* Psychology Today. https://www.psychologytoday.com/intl/blog/me-we/201312/10-sources-low-self-esteem

LaMotte, S. (2021, November 27). *CBT: A way to reshape your negative thinking and reduce stress.* CNN. https://edition.cnn.com/2021/11/27/health/cbt-cognitive-behavioral-therapy-wellness/index.html

LePera, Nicole. (2022). *How to meet your self: The workbook for self-discovery.* HarperCollins.

Manson, M. (2016). *The subtle art of not giving a fuck : A counterintuitive approach to living a good life.* Harperone.

Mayo Clinic. (2018, May 4). *Anxiety disorders.* https://www.mayoclinic.org/diseases-conditions/anxiety/symptoms-causes/syc-20350961

Mayo Clinic. (2022, February 3). *Positive thinking: Stop negative self-talk to reduce stress.* https://www.mayoclinic.org/healthy-lifestyle/stress-management/in-depth/positive-thinking/art-20043950

Medical News Today. (2020, March 31). *Grounding techniques for anxiety, PTSD, and trauma.* https://www.medicalnewstoday.com/articles/g rounding-techniques#seeing-a-doctor

Millacci, T. (2017, February 28). *What is gratitude and why is it so important?* PositivePsychology.com. https://positivepsychology.com/gratitude-appreciation/

Naik, D. (2022, January 4). *Twelve ways to build a great support system.* Mintlounge. https://lifestyle.livemint.com/health/wellness/ twelve-ways-to-build-a-great-support-system-111641264593251.html

Porges, S. W. (2011). *The polyvagal theory: Neurophysiological foundations of emotions, attachment, communication, and self-regulation.* Norton.

Renouf, A. G., & Harter, S. (1990). Low self-worth and anger as components of the depressive experience in young adolescents. *Development and Psychopathology, 2(3),* 293–310. https://doi.org/10.1017/s095457940000078x

Richter, S. S., Brown, S. A., & Mott, M. A. (1991). The impact of social support and self-esteem on adolescent substance abuse treatment outcome. *Journal of Substance Abuse, 3(4),* 371–385.

https://doi.org/10.1016/s0899-3289(10)80019-7

Rogers, C. R. (1961). *On Becoming a Person: A Therapist's View of Psychotherapy.* Houghton Mifflin, C.

Ronin, K. (2020, June 19). *9 myths about confidence that are holding you back.* The Muse. https://www.themuse.com/advice/9-myths-about-confidence-that-are-holding-you-back

Santarossa, S., & Woodruff, S. J. (2017). #SocialMedia: Exploring the relationship of social networking sites on body image, self-esteem, and eating disorders. *Social Media + Society, 3*(2), 1–10. https://doi.org/10.1177/2056305117704407

Sharaf, A. Y., Thompson, E. A., & Walsh, E. (2009). Protective effects of self-esteem and family support on suicide risk behaviors among at-risk adolescents. *Journal of Child and Adolescent Psychiatric Nursing, 22*(3), 160–168. https://doi.org/10.1111/j.1744-6171.2009.00194.x

Smith, J. (2022). *Why has nobody told me this before?* Michael Joseph Ltd.

Sowislo, J. F., & Orth, U. (2013). Does low self-esteem predict depression and anxiety? A meta-analysis of longitudinal studies. *Psychological Bulletin,*

139(1), 213–240. https://doi.org/10.1037/a0028931

Stevenson, J., & Osborne, M. (Directors). (2008, June 6). *Kung fu panda* [Film]. DreamWorks Animation.

The Attachment Project. (2023, April 6). *Attachment styles & their role in our adult relationships.* https://www.attachmentproject.com/blog/four-attachment-styles/

Trenton, N. (2021). *Stop overthinking : 23 techniques to relieve stress, stop negative spirals, declutter your mind, and focus on the present.* PKCS Media.

Tulshyan, R., & Burey, J.-A. (2021, February 11). *Stop telling women they have imposter syndrome.* Harvard Business Review. https://hbr.org/2021/02/stop-telling-women-they-have-imposter-syndrome

van der Kolk, B. (2014). *The body keeps the score: Mind, brain and body in the transformation of trauma.* Penguin Books.

Weber, J. P. (2019, June 21). *4 myths about self-esteem: The first myth? You either have self-esteem or you don't.* Psychology Today. https://www.psychologytoday.com/intl/blog/

having-sex-wanting-intimacy/201906/4-myths-about-self-esteem

Whiting, J. (2016, July 21). *Eight reasons women stay in abusive relationships*. Institute for Family Studies. https://ifstudies.org/blog/eight-reasons-women-stay-in-abusive-relationships

Winfield, A. (2015, January 15). *Perfectionism and self-esteem*. Mindfully Well Counselling Cork. https://corkpsychotherapyandtraumacentre.ie/self-esteem/perfectionism-self-esteem/

Printed in Great Britain
by Amazon